Fatherhood is a cornerstone of the family—and the family is a cornerstone of civilization. I love being a father and a husband, and having a close and loving family is one of the greatest blessings a man can know. Yet fathers—and families—are falling apart at rates we have never seen before in America. And our Nation's children are paying the price. That's why I'm glad my friend Gregory Slayton has written this hands-on, no-holds-barred, gut-level-honest book. *Be a Better Dad Today!* is the result of Gregory's multi-year study of fatherhood on five different continents and his 20-plus years as a father of four great kids. This is a book for every man who wants to be a better father, a better husband and a better man. I highly recommend it.

Sam Brownback, Governor of Kansas

Gregory Slayton had to learn to be a great father to his kids without his own dad's help. In this book, he gives you tools that will empower you to do the most important job you will ever have as a man. It's a very practical and hopeful book.

Jim Burns, Ph.D., President, HomeWord
Author of *10 Building Blocks for a Solid Family* and *Teenology: The Art of Raising Great Teens*

Having been raised by a man who exemplified what it means to be a great father, I am blessed to have learned from one of the greatest. In *Be a Better Dad Today!* Gregory explains how to navigate the most important job in the world. This book is a great resource for today's dads or those who plan to be a dad in the future.

Jeb Bush, Former Governor of Florida (1999–2007)

There is no more important job in the world for men than being a good father for our kids. I love being a dad—and I always have. That's why I appreciate the honesty, the humor and the many helpful ideas that my friend Gregory Slayton has packed into *Be a Better Dad Today!* Being a better dad today—and every day of our lives—is one of the most important things we can do for our family, our community and our nation.

G. K. Butterfield, United States Congressman

Be a Better Dad Today! engages us as men with wisdom, joy and honest understanding of the challenges we face. Gregory reminds us that we are literally irreplaceable in our roles as husband and father—and that these are the most important jobs we will ever have. The Ten Tools of Fatherhood will be helpful to each and every man who puts them to work.

Dr. Patrick P. Gelsinger, President and COO, EMC Corporation
Author of *The Juggling Act*

I have known Gregory for 30 years, and he is passionate, practical and visionary. His book is all three of those things and more. As a father of five, I highly recommend *Be a Better Dad Today!* to all dads—and dads to be—of any age.

Hans Helmerich, President and CEO, Helmerich and Payne

Be a Better Dad Today! is perhaps the most practical and down-to-earth manual you will find on how to be an effective father. You will not be able to read it without being both spiritually convicted and personally equipped.

Tim Keller, Senior Pastor, Redeemer Presbyterian Church, New York City

Gregory Slayton writes eloquently about the God-given nobility of fatherhood, an institution of grand personal, familial and societal importance, but also a journey that many men embark on without fully knowing the true path or destination. Slayton deepens our understanding of what being a father means and offers guidance on how fathers can realize their fullest potential.

Joe Lieberman, United States Senator

I learned about life and honor from my father and grandfather, who were my heroes as Naval officers and, most importantly, fathers. Earning their respect was the most lasting ambition of my life, and even though they are no longer with us, I continue to live my life according to the terms of their approval. Their courage and faith were an inspiration to me and a key to my survival in some of my most difficult times. I am grateful for the memories of these two great men and the respect and affection they provided as the patriarchs of our family. I've personally known Gregory and his family for years, and I know he exemplifies the title of his book *Be a Better Dad Today!* each and every day of his life. There are certain lessons in life that can best be taught by fathers. My hope is that this book will help every single man who picks it up to be the best father, the best husband, and the best man he can be.

John McCain, United States Senator

Leslie and I founded the Center for Relationship Development on the campus of Seattle Pacific University almost 20 years ago. During those 20 years, we have seen firsthand the critical importance of the fathering skills that Gregory lays out so clearly in *Be a Better Dad Today!* If you want to be a better father, a better husband and a better man, this book will help you on that path.

Les Parrott, Ph.D., LesandLeslie.com; Author of *Crazy Good Sex*

All over the world, the family is in deep trouble. It is just as much a reality in countries like Argentina and China as it is in the United States and Great Britain. It is becoming even more challenging for today's modern Christian father to lead and protect his family. And, sadly, some have even given up. *Be a Better Dad Today!* shows each of us men how to be the best father, the best husband, and indeed the best man we can be—all in light of our relationship with our heavenly Father. We all need that kind of encouragement, strength and wisdom . . . today and every day of our lives.

Luis Palau, World Evangelist

As a senior executive with a growing family, I know firsthand the challenges of being both a good dad and a good manager in today's world. That's why I am so thankful for *Be a Better Dad Today!* My good friend Gregory Slayton is a great father himself and has made a 30-year study of good fathers around the world. He has used that unique background to write a great, practical, hands-on book that will be a real blessing to every father or father-to-be who reads it. I highly recommend *Be a Better Dad Today!* to any man who wants to improve his fathering skills—and have fun doing it.

Sanjay Poonen, President and Corporate Officer, Global Solutions, SAP

All dads need help to be the best fathers they can be. The health of our families, our culture and our civilization literally depend on it. My friend Gregory Slayton has written a great book that will help every man who reads it be the best dad he can be. *Be a Better Dad Today!* is a truly enjoyable, deeply practical and immensely helpful book for men everywhere. As a father, a pastor and a man who wants to be the very best I can be, I highly recommend it.

Rev. Samuel Rodriguez, President, National Hispanic Christian Leadership Conference (The Hispanic Evangelical Association)

As the team pastor for the Houston Texans, a happily married husband for 30 years and the proud father of three adult children, I understand that solid communication is essential to developing a winning team. Just as a team looks to the quarterback for leadership and guidance, our families look to dads to valiantly lead and guide them through the obstacle courses of life. *Be a Better Dad Today!* will help every dad become a better teammate, a better husband, a better father and a better man! Just like All-Pro athletes, All-Pro fathers are made, not born. Read this book and start training today!

Greg Tyler, Team Pastor, Houston Texans

When I speak with fathers—and I speak to lots of them—they often ask me, "What do I need to do to be a better dad?" Well, Gregory Slayton's book certainly helps answer this important question. Filled with personal stories and practical advice and strategies, *Be a Better Dad Today!* is a much-needed resource that I highly recommend any dad to have in his library.

Roland C. Warren, President, National Fatherhood Initiative Germantown, Maryland

As a former college and NFL quarterback, I've had the privilege of playing with some great teams. But as a father, there is no team more important to me than my family. And that's why this book is so important. *Be a Better Dad Today!* can help every dad become an All-Pro father. The book's Ten Tools of Fatherhood are exactly what we need as dads to sharpen and expand our fatherhood skills. And Gregory gets it exactly right when he says that no matter what else we do as men, fatherhood is our most important job. I highly recommend this book to every man who wants to be a better dad, a better husband and a better man.

Danny Wuerffel, Executive Director of Desire Street Ministries

SPECIAL CHUCK COLSON EDITION

GREGORY W. SLAYTON

BE A
BETTER
DAD
TODAY!

10 TOOLS EVERY FATHER NEEDS

Regal

From Gospel Light
Ventura, California, U.S.A.

Published by Regal
From Gospel Light
Ventura, California, U.S.A.
www.regalbooks.com
Printed in the U.S.A.

Scripture quotations are taken from the following:

Slayton, Gregory.
The Library of Congress has catalogued the first edition as follows:
Be a better dad today! : ten tools every father needs / Gregory Slayton.
p. cm.
ISBN 978-0-8307-6207-1 (hardcover)
1. Fatherhood—Religious aspects—Christianity. I. Title.
BV4529.17.S53 2012
248.8′421—dc23
2011045676

Rights for publishing this book outside the U.S.A. or in non-English
languages are administered by Gospel Light Worldwide, an international not-
for-profit ministry. For additional information, please visit www.glww.org,
email info@glww.org, or write to Gospel Light Worldwide, 1957 Eastman
Avenue, Ventura, CA 93003, U.S.A.

To order copies of this book and other Regal products in bulk quantities,
please contact us at 1-800-446-7735.

Contents

PART ONE: The Journey of a Lifetime

PART TWO: The Ten Tools of Fatherhood

Part Three: Special Situations

FOREWORD

To call Gregory Slayton's life "full" would be an understatement. He spent much of his twenties helping people throughout the developing world: He was a Fulbright Scholar to Asia, ran an orphanage in Manila, spearheaded micro-credit programs in southeast Asia, and was a World Vision regional manager in West Africa.

In his thirties, he became a leader in the rise of Silicon Valley, both as a master of turning good ideas into very profitable ones and as a venture capitalist. His work was the basis for a number of case studies at the Harvard Business School.

He followed that season of life by becoming a diplomat. He was named the United States Consul General and Chief of Mission to Bermuda by President George W. Bush. His work made him the first Republican in history to receive the Distinguished Foreign Service Award from members of the Congressional Black Caucus.

Yet it is clear to anyone who knows Slayton that all of these accomplishments pale in comparison to his commitment to Christ and his love for his family. It is these commitments that lie behind *Be a Better Dad Today!*

When Slayton calls fatherhood "the most important job in the world," he is not mouthing a greeting card platitude. He knows the difference that a father's absence can make in the life of a child.

As do I. The past three decades have given me a close-up look at the consequences of the collapse of the family in the twentieth century and into the twenty-first century. In my visits to 800 prisons, I have seen what happens to many kids who have no dads: Looking for male role models, which all boys need, they turn to the gangs.

At first I thought that turning these young men around would be a simple matter, such as building discipleship groups. But what I soon discovered was that we were building prisons faster than Prison Fellowship or anyone else could get to them. So I started studying the causes of crime. I read Richard J. Herrnstein and James Q. Wilson's *Crime and Human Nature*, which, in a nutshell, says that crime is caused by the lack of moral training in the morally formative years.

This should not come as a surprise to Christians. After all, Proverbs 22:6 tells us to "train a child in the way he should go, and when he is old he will not turn from it" (*NIV*). Yet, if you look at our prisons, it is clear that many children are not receiving that training—not because their mothers didn't try to teach them right from wrong, but because that kind of training requires a mother *and* a father.

The link between crime and fatherlessness is undeniable, as are the links between the lack of a father and a whole host of what social scientists call "adverse outcomes." Yet our society persists in treating family formation and structure as something malleable that can be shaped to suit our predilections.

Gregory Slayton knows better. That is why he calls being a father "the most important job in the world." It is why he started an online community for American Dads called Fellowship of Fathers. It is why he wrote *Be a Better Day Today!*

What you are about to read isn't theory—it is every bit as practical as it is vital. It is the kind of thing that can change lives and communities.

Charles W. Colson

Founder, Prison Fellowship and the Chuck Colson Center for Christian Worldview

INTRODUCTION

The Most Important Job a Man Will Ever Have

Thank you for picking up this book. The fact that you did tells me you want to be a better dad. And that means you and I have something very important in common.

Being a good father isn't easy, and there is no instruction manual. It's pretty much a 24/7 labor of love—love that isn't always returned. But it is absolutely the most important job you and I will ever have. Perhaps you are a father who hasn't done such a great job in the past. Don't lose hope. You can still be a good father in the future, and I will tell you how in this book. None of us are perfect fathers. We are fathers who are learning how to be the best parents we can be, and that takes time and practice. Admitting that you have failed in your role as a father, or realizing you didn't have the skills to be a good father, is a great place to begin.

If you doubt me on that last point, think about it: Not only does the future of civilization depend on how we collectively do our job (and that is no exaggeration), but also our children's future, our family's future and our own future depend on it as well. In the thousands of years before our modern TV/Internet culture, mothers and fathers understood implicitly that the job they did as parents was critical to their future and society's future. And while some today may try to de-emphasize the importance of effective parenting, there is no better "return on investment" than children who grow up to be a blessing to their families and an asset to the world. As Peter Lynch, cofounder of Fidelity Investments, has said repeatedly: Children are our best investment . . . by far.

For more than 30 years now, I have had the privilege of studying fathers and fatherhood in widely different societies and cultures around the world. In every part of the world, at all times, fatherhood matters more than almost anything else. The fact is that children who grow up without their dads here in the United States are two to three times more likely to spend time in prison, become addicted to drugs, fail out of high school, have children themselves out of wedlock, suffer from mental illness, and die an early, violent death.[1] So, yes, being a good dad is vitally important. In fact, in chapter 1 we're going to look at the importance of fatherhood for our families, our society and ourselves. I hope that by the time we're done, you will understand the many reasons why being a good dad is the most important job any of us—from the President of the United States to the CEO of a major corporation to the guy taking out the garbage—will ever have.

Some cultures and countries do a good job of affirming, guiding and encouraging fathers. Modern American culture is sadly lacking in these areas—and we are all poorer for it. But the good news is this: Good dads are *made* . . . not born. How do I know this? Because I didn't have a real dad—the kind of dad I'm writing about—growing up. He was more of an absentee father early on, and then completely disappeared. Maybe you also didn't have great role models when you were young. Many of us did not. And I've certainly made more than my share of parenting mistakes—maybe we have that in common as well.

But I have some very good news for you: I am 100 percent sure that together, if we put our hearts, minds and souls into it, and with God's help, we can become better fathers. Starting today.

The Noble Family Vision and the Ten Tools of Fatherhood

Becoming the best dads we can be is the journey of a lifetime. And, as with any great journey, we need three important things. First, we need a map of where we are trying to go. This "map" is really a vision of what type of dad we want to be and what kind of family we want to have in 5, 10, 20 years . . . and how we are going to make that vision reality. Second, we need a strong set of tools to help us get there. And third, we also need a few key people to journey with us and help us when times get really tough.

The map for your fatherhood journey is what I call your "Noble Family Vision." This is a map of the future to which you are trying to lead your loved ones. This Noble Family Vision, which we will look at in chapter 2, will help you envision the type of father—and the type of family—you want to become. As with any good map, it will be important for you to look at your Noble Family Vision from time to time. But it will be especially important when the storms and trials of life set in, when you aren't sure about the way forward, or when you are just flat-out lost. Each of those things is certain to happen, because the fatherhood journey is a real-life journey. However, if you have a Noble Family Vision in place, it can help get you back on the right path.

Of course, by itself, even the best map in the world is useless. This is why in addition to a Noble Family Vision you also need the right set of tools for your fatherhood journey. These tools, each of which we will examine in detail in Part Two of this book, are transforming in nature because they are rooted in faith, hope and love—which, when combined, have the power to change lives. As the Bible reminds us, even in the deepest and darkest moments, "love never fails" (1 Corinthians 13:8). Faith, hope and love transform lives. The Ten Tools of Fatherhood are based on timeless biblical values and principles that have stood for thousands of years. I have seen that power at work in my own life—and in the lives of men and women in different cultures, nations and people groups in the world. And they will work for you.

Every dad can master these 10 tools and become a much better father. But you can't master them alone. Just like you didn't teach yourself geometry or how to read, you'll need help. First and foremost, you will need the help of your wife or partner, even if you are no longer together. She will be your biggest ally on this journey. Let me tell you a secret: She will be thrilled to help you, because no one in this world loves your children more than she does. Please don't put this book down if you're a single dad. I absolutely do not advocate divorce or having children outside of marriage, but, as they say, "life happens." That's why I've dedicated an entire chapter in Part Three on the importance of being the best single dad you can be. So please, read on, brother.

Most mothers realize instinctively that they need a strong and effective father figure to properly raise their children. If you are married, don't despair if your marriage isn't everything you'd like it to be; no one's marriage is, because all marriages are made up of two flawed human beings. You can learn to strengthen your marriage partnership with your wife, and together you can raise wonderful children.

In addition to a strong partnership with your children's mother, whether she is your wife or not, you will also need the help of other good dads. Very few journeys of real significance are accomplished alone. Whether it is a football team's journey to the Superbowl or an individual's quest to conquer a personal addiction, it takes the support of a strong and committed team of friends to succeed. To become a great father, you need the assistance, encouragement and support of other good dads. Don't worry if you don't yet have those kinds of buddies. Our Fellowship of Fathers network stretches around the world, and no matter where you are, you can be a part of a great group of men.

Finally, even with a clear map, the right tools and people to help, you will need one more thing on your journey: a strong dose of God's grace. Each of us will make mistakes along the way—I've made plenty—but fortunately, God's grace is available to all. As both the Old and New Testaments tell us, God's desire is "to turn the hearts of the fathers back to their children . . . and the hearts of the children back to their fathers" (Malachi 4:6). I believe that Scripture is His desire for us today as individuals and as a culture overall. In fact, that is why I wrote this book.

Getting the Most Out of this Book

My goal is that this isn't just a normal book for you. If this is a book that you read through once, get excited about for a short time, and then forget about a few months later, it will be a failure for both of us. Instead, my prayer is that this book (and the highlighted wisdom, web services and tools found at www.Fellow shipOfFathers.com) will help you to make real, ongoing progress on your Fatherhood Journey for many years to come. (I realize that in some situations, Internet access may be limited or available only for short amounts of time. We hope that when you do have access, you'll make contacting us, even briefly, a priority.)

While www.FellowshipofFathers.com is a "members only" site, the good news is that you are now a charter member just for buying this book (or getting it as a gift). The entire site is a clearinghouse of the very best fatherhood tools, ideas and services that should prove extremely helpful to you as a dad. You can also interact with other fathers from your area—or around the world—who may be facing similar challenges at www.facebook.com/BeaBetter DadToday. You will be able to get good, confidential advice and support from older dads who have "been there, done that." And you will be able to share with us your insights and ideas on fatherhood, which I know will be helpful.

Most of us tend to overestimate what we can get done in one year and we underestimate what we can get done in 10 or 20 years *if* we really put our hearts into it. Raising a happy, healthy family is a multi-year process that has plenty of challenges. Sure, there will be setbacks and sometimes some big disappointments, but "two steps forward, one step back" is the way of this world. Rome wasn't built in a day—and neither are great dads or strong and loving families.

So, I hope this will be a book that you read slowly—to get the most out of every chapter—and go back to whenever you need encouragement or some new ideas on the fatherhood front. I also hope that we have the chance to get to know each other at www.face book.com/BeaBetterDadToday. I look forward to your ideas, thoughts and suggestions. Like any team, the Fellowship of Fathers is stronger together. I pray this book helps us *both* to become much better dads—today and every day, for the rest of our lives.

That's the main reason I wrote this book. In fact, that's the *only* reason I wrote this book. I am passionate about the importance of fatherhood, not only for our families and our society but also for our own development as men. Fatherhood is not a sprint; it's the journey of a lifetime, and on it you will discover the man you were always meant to be. I know that with the right tools, the right help and the right heart, you and I can both be better dads today and every day going forward. That is incredibly worthwhile. In fact, it's the most important journey you and I will ever take.

So thanks for beginning this journey of discovery. And thanks for your willingness to do some soul-searching and to commit to heartfelt honesty on the journey.

As one great dad said on 9/11, "Let's roll!"

If you would like to discuss any of this material via email, feel free to contact me at **gws@beabetterdadtoday.com**

Note

1. *Father Facts,* fifth edition, National Fatherhood Initiative, 2007. http://www.father hood.org/organizations/programs/father-facts/overview.

A PERSONAL STORY:

A Good Father

Before we begin, I want to share a personal story with you to explain why fatherhood means so much to me. I didn't have much of a dad growing up. I do have some good memories of him when I was very young, but over time, alcohol and other destructive habits took him farther and farther from our family. He and my mother divorced when I was a young man. It was not pretty. Then my dad cut himself off completely from my brothers and me.

The last time I spoke with my father was 25 years ago. I was in the hospital with acute viral hepatitis, which I had contracted while living and working on the great plains of Africa (that's a story in its own right . . . but one for another book). I was very ill, near death in fact. One day, my father called me on the phone in my room at the hospital (I was only semi-conscious at the time). He and I spoke for a few minutes, during which he talked mostly about himself. Despite his multi-year absence, it was good to hear from him. Then, a few minutes into our conversation, he said something I will never forget: "I've got to go. I'll call you back." No explanation, no discussion, just a dead phone line.

For 20-plus years, I never heard from him—until one day my brother got a call from a fellow attorney who had found his name on the Internet. Our father was dead. He had died poor, alone and in great pain. But because he had cut himself off from his family, we were powerless to help him. And the things he had counted on throughout his life (like money and power) had completely failed him. Ultimately, he had lived for himself, and he had died by himself. He reaped exactly what he had sown. He was one of the saddest men I have ever known.

To say that he was not a good dad would be an understatement, but that's not the point. I'm sure that some of you reading this book had childhoods that were much tougher. I grew up in relative affluence, and (thanks to my mom and Dartmouth College) I got a very good education. My mother tried her best to provide a good home, and I will always love her for that. But my home was not a happy one.

Fortunately, I was lucky enough to have a very close friend growing up. Ken Chang and his family lived a few miles from our home, but we were inseparable. We had moved into the same town within a few years of each other and had quickly formed an enduring friendship. Ken came from a Chinese background; in fact, his paternal grandfather had worked for Chiang Kai-shek (the first president of Taiwan). But Ken and his whole family were Christians—in fact, they were very strong and faithful believers. Ken's maternal grandfather had been the first one in his village in southern China to become a Christian when missionaries from Hudson Taylor's China Inland Mission visited his village. Through the generations, the family had remained faithful believers. And they welcomed me with warmth and kindness.

Ken's father was a quiet, hard-working man who loved his family very much. He spent most of his days running the local store they owned. He was a calm and loving leader for his family in good times and bad—a good man in word and deed. Spending as much time as I did in Ken's home made me acutely aware of the stark differences between his father and mine. To Mr. Chang, fatherhood mattered. A lot. And it still does. His example of servant leadership continues to be a motivation for me today. His good work as a dad was proof positive to me that you don't need to be wealthy, well educated or come from the "right" family to be a good dad. He was a good father, and he helped his son, Ken, become a very good man and an excellent father himself (with a very, very good wife). The blessings that Grandfather Chang started were clearly passed on to his son. And his son, Ken's dad, continued the cycle of blessing as a strong and faithful father. Ken has continued to pass those blessings down to his children.

So it is to good fathers everywhere—like my friend Ken and his father and grandfather—that this book is dedicated.

PART ONE

The Journey of a Lifetime

1

The Importance of Fatherhood

Fatherhood is the most important job that any of us—including the President of the United States or the CEO of the world's largest company—will ever have. It is the only role in life for which we are truly indispensable. Our futures, our family and our entire society depend on the job we do as a dad.

I would never have become half the man I am without the help, the support and the leadership of my dad. He taught me how to be a real man.
DAVE H., BOSTON, MASSACHUSETTS

Nothing I've ever done has given me more joys and rewards than being a father to my children.
BILL COSBY

If you would like to discuss any of this material via email, feel free to contact me at **gws@beabetterdadtoday.com**

Somehow, much of our society has forgotten this simple fact that Bill Cosby expressed so well in the quote on the previous page. Down through history, men have gotten great joy from being good fathers, and society has directly benefited. Fatherhood has always been one of the cornerstones of civilization. In fact, many of the most serious social issues our society wrestles with (from adult illiteracy to teenage pregnancy to increasing rates of chronic unemployment, drug abuse and mental illness) stem directly from the breakdown of fatherhood.

The statistics are abundantly clear: Children who grow up without fathers are two to three times more likely to spend time in jail, drop out of school, fail to ever hold down a long-term job, suffer from a severe mental illness, or become addicted to drugs or alcohol. And they are three to four times more likely to bear children out of wedlock themselves . . . and thus continue the cycle of social devastation that threatens our society.[1]

Of course, the presence or absence of a good mother is also important in the life of every child. While I do not want to downplay the extraordinary importance of mothers, this book is dedicated to men just like you—men who want to be strong and noble fathers for their families, and have fun doing it. I share that goal with you, and an exciting one it is! We are on a journey—you and I—and it won't be completed this side of eternity. Becoming a good father is like running a marathon; it takes time, dedication and sticking to it. In addition, like all important journeys, we will never arrive if we don't know where we are going. The fact that we share an important goal—to be strong and noble fathers—is an excellent start.

Maybe you're thinking, *Well, that's a good idea, but a bit old-fashioned for the twenty-first century.* Or maybe you're feeling burdened by what you perceive as your failures as a father. Or maybe you're just starting out on this whole fatherhood thing and you're not really sure how it works. All good questions and valid feelings, for we have all failed at one time or another, we have all had questions about the future, and our society today vastly underestimates the importance of fathers. So, if you are a father, or even if you're just thinking about becoming a father, you are in (or about to start) the most important job of your life.

Why Is This Job So Important?

You and I will probably have many jobs in our work careers—that is the way of the modern world. A few jobs may be great, a couple will be horrible, but all will come to an end (and some will come to an end sooner than we would like). If we are deeply honest with ourselves, none of us is truly irreplaceable in our professional jobs. That's not an insult—it's reality.

Among my other roles so far I have been a CEO, a venture capitalist, an ambassador and a college professor. (I've also been unemployed, but more on that in the chapter titled "How to Handle Life's Beanballs.") In every role I have ever had—even in roles in which I have won awards or achieved marked success—I knew there were others out there who would probably do as good a job, or maybe even a better one, than me. But in my job as a dad to my children, like all dads for their kids, I cannot be replaced.

The same is true of you as well. You are the best-qualified person in the entire world for that job. There is no one else—no one—who has the emotional, spiritual and physical assets you bring to this job. No other man will ever love your children as much as you do (and I know you love your kids, or you wouldn't be reading this book). No other man is in the spiritual and emotional position to understand your kids as well as you do. And no other man is likely to be as committed to helping your kids build a successful future as you are. For them, you cannot be replaced.

Not only are you the very best person in the world for this job, but it is also the most important job you will ever have. The statistics are clear: The lives of your children will be hugely impacted by the job you do as their dad—and not only the lives of your children, but of their children and their children's children.

What other job will you hold that will ever bring you so much happiness over such a long period of time (the rest of your life)? What other job can so impact the wider world? Just consider the example of

A Story from the White House

I have been privileged to know a number of U.S. Presidents personally—some better than others. And no matter what you thought of him as a President, George W. Bush was—and is—an exceptional father. He knows a deep secret that all great dads know: Being a good father and a faithful husband is as much of a blessing for him as it is for his wife and daughters. He understands that learning how to be a good dad has helped him to be a better man in many important ways.

Once, early in his first term as President at a beautiful evening event at the White House, he took me aside, looked me right in the eyes and said, "Gregory, you and I have a lot in common: We both married way above ourselves. Don't ever forget that." I understood that as a reminder to always love and honor my wife—something he told me more than once. That was very good advice then, and it still is today. But then he went on to say something even more profound: "Becoming a husband and then a dad is one of the best things that ever happened to me—because it forced me to be a better man than I was." The President certainly had it right. It is in bearing the burdens of family and fatherhood that our inner man grows stronger.

Albert Einstein—he was a scientific genius, but he didn't think he would have gotten there without the early guidance and help of his father. And what other job pays such important dividends for future generations? Being a good father today will impact your descendants to the third and fourth generation . . . and possibly beyond.

That's right, your influence as a father goes beyond just your own children and grandchildren; it impacts society now and for generations to come. So, as a job that will last a lifetime, hold many rewards, and have almost an unlimited potential for benefiting you, your family and others long into the future, I hope you will agree with me that being a dad is the most important job you and I (or the President of the United States) will ever have.

But, being a good dad isn't only vital for the future of our families and our society; it is also critical to our own development as men.

A Vital Step in Our Development as Men

How do gold medal Olympic weight lifters become so strong? How did Jamaican sprinter Usain "Lightning" Bolt become the fastest man in the world? How does a team become Superbowl champions? Believe it or not, the same way you and I become good fathers (and, in the process, much better men).

Self-sacrifice, hard work and self-discipline are some of the key building blocks to becoming a champion athlete and a championship team. These qualities are also the building blocks of champion dads of loving families. Research has long shown that men who are committed husbands and fathers are on average more productive in their jobs, enjoy better mental health, are generally happier with their lives, and contribute more to their communities than their unmarried or childless brothers.[2] In fact, married people are twice as likely to be "happy" with life, and less than half as likely to be "not too happy" compared to either single, cohabiting, separated, divorced or widowed people.[3]

However, there is something else profoundly important about the fatherhood journey. As long as we don't give up on ourselves, or our families, we are changed into better men through the refining fire of being a father.

Let's face it: Who wants to get up at 2:00 AM to make their pregnant wife the pickle sandwich she is craving? Who wants to take baby for the umpteenth stroll in the baby carriage so Mom can get a short (and much needed) break? Who wants to clean up after a sick child, or change the bed linens after a messy sleepover, or discipline a teen who desperately needs it? In short, no one except those who seek to be champion dads.

Likewise, who wants to get up every day at 5:00 AM to run 5 or 10 miles? Who wants to do two-a-day workouts in pre-season? Who wants to push their bodies to their physical limit so they can become stronger, faster and better at their chosen sport? Again, the answer is no one except those who wish to become champion athletes.

That's the rub: There is no shortcut to becoming a champion athlete, just as there is no shortcut to becoming a good father and a good man. The very burdens that we carry for our families over time and the weight on our shoulders that can sometimes seem almost crushing are what make us better dads and stronger men. That is one of the deepest secrets of fatherhood. Not only do our family members—and our society as a whole—benefit tremendously from the process of our becoming good dads, but you and I, brother, benefit as well. Again, the research backs this up. Data shows that mental health generally improves after marriage and deteriorates after divorce or separation. Furthermore, this research has shown that these effects occur as a result of marriage and divorce and are not due to other factors.[4]

Let's Take This Journey Together

Unfortunately, our society has de-emphasized the importance of fathers and fatherhood during the past 50 years, and we are much the worse for it. A man's career success or his sexual prowess or the size of his car or boat or bank account are all considered, in different circles, more important than his success as a father. This is incredibly shortsighted, for the importance of all of those things will fade long before we exit this world, and they will mean nothing at all after our death. If heaven exists (as I strongly believe it does), faith, family and friendship will mean everything, while material stuff will mean nothing.

Unfortunately, in our modern age advertising is everywhere, and it tries to focus our attention each and every day on the material. But while there is nothing inherently wrong with career success or material possessions, we must keep those goals in balance with the other, much more important, goals on our life journey. That is not easy to do, especially in the twenty-first century.

Sadly, our culture provides precious little support, guidance or encouragement for fathers, even though the future of our society depends on the institution of fatherhood. That is why I wrote this book. I needed more help, more encouragement, more good ideas and great suggestions from fellow dads like you. And I suspected that there were more than a few fellow fathers who felt the same way.

So, I hope you now agree with me about the supreme importance of fatherhood for our families, our society and for ourselves. I would like us to share our fatherhood journey and encourage and strengthen one another for the road ahead. It is my hope that this book and the web tools and services that are at your disposal will be an effective toolset for you as you tackle the many challenges of being a good father.

Even though my wife and I have raised four wonderful kids and I have been a lifelong student of fatherhood, I have a lot more to learn from you. So log on to www.facebook.com/Be aBetterDad Today now and give me your personal feedback on this chapter and what you hope to get out of this book. I'm excited about joining you on this greatest of all of life's journeys.

For Further Reflection

1. Do you truly believe in your heart that being a father is the most important job you will ever have? Why or why not?

2. How would you rate yourself as a father today, on a 1 to 10 scale (with 1 as the best)? Would your children's mother and kids agree with that rating? Do you have the courage to ask them?

3. What would you say are your greatest opportunities for improvement as a dad? What would your children's mother and your kids say?

Today's Quick Wins

1. Take 60 seconds to reflect on this fact: For each of your children, and for your entire family, you cannot be replaced.

2. Take 60 seconds to think about the extent of your power, for good or for evil, over your family's future.

3. Take 60 seconds to meditate on how you, single-handedly, can (and will) shape the future of your children and your family . . . and the influence they will have on their society and generations to come because of you.

Notes

1. *Father Facts*, fifth edition, National Fatherhood Initiative, 2007. http://www.fatherhood.org/organizations/programs/father-facts/overview.
2. Linda J. Waite and Maggie Gallagher, *The Case for Marriage* (New York: Doubleday, 2000).
3. Ibid.
4. Alex Bierman, Elena M. Fazio and Melissa A. Milkie, "A Multifaceted Approach to the Mental Health Advantage of the Married: Assessing How Explanations Vary by Outcome Measure and Unmarried Group," *Journal of Family Issues*, vol. 27, no. 4, April 2006, midus.wisc.edu/findings/pdfs/281.pdf.

The Power of a "Noble Family Vision"

A Noble Family Vision is like a roadmap of what you and your family want to be like in 10 or 20 or 30 years. Having one can be the difference between getting there safe and sound . . . or not.

Where there is no vision, the people perish.
PROVERBS 29:18, *KJV*

Getting on the same page with my wife and kids about what we wanted our family to be in the future, and why, was one of the best things we ever did.
JOHN C., SEATTLE, WASHINGTON

If you would like to discuss any of this material via email, feel free to contact me at **gws@beabetterdadtoday.com**

Leo Tolstoy, one of the greatest of the great Russian writers, started one of the world's most famous novels, *Anna Karenina*, with a haunting observation: "Happy families resemble one another, whereas each unhappy family is unhappy in its own tragic way."

Almost 150 years later, Tolstoy's observation still rings true. And I will add a another truth: "Happy families are not built by accident." Of that I am 100 percent sure. Strong, loving, caring families are built over time, memory by memory, in good times and (not infrequently) tough times. But what can keep us going as men, as the leaders of our families, especially when the winds and the tides of life seem to blow and pull against us?

How can we, as fathers, set the tone and establish the direction for our families, while ensuring that we get every family member moving as a team in that direction? It all starts with what I call a Noble Family Vision.

Leadership Sets the Tone and Determines the Outcome

General Dwight D. Eisenhower knew that the Allied invasion of Nazi-occupied Europe was going to be a bloody mess. Thousands of men would die, tens of thousands would be wounded and an Allied victory was uncertain, at best. The weather and the seas did not cooperate. At times, even his Allies did not cooperate. But Ike had a vision—a Noble Vision—for a democratic and prosperous Europe free of Nazi tyranny. Ike understood the importance of that vision—he understood that the future of the free world depended on it. He made sure that all of his team, from his senior staff on down, understood the importance of that vision. He also made sure that every member of his staff understood their role in the fulfillment of that vision.

Bringing that vision to reality required enormous sacrifice, tremendous discipline and superb teamwork. But Ike did not waver—and his team did not falter. They understood the vision, and they understood the huge human cost if they failed. Because they understood these things and stuck to them through thick and thin, Europe was freed of Nazi socialism and has enjoyed relative peace and prosperity for six-plus decades. Ike's noble vision came to pass—and we are all the better for it.

And therein is my first—and maybe most important—question for you: What is your "Noble Vision" for your family? In other words, what do you want your family to look like in 5 years, 10 years, 20 years? And what are you, as the leader of your family, doing to advance that goal?

What's that? You don't have a Noble Vision for your family's future? Or perhaps you have a bit of a vision, but you've never shared it with your family? My friend, welcome to the club. Most of us dads are so busy providing for our families and taking care of daily challenges that we haven't taken time to truly think about what we would like our families to be in the future. And that is a problem, because nothing of any human significance is ever built by accident.

Think about it. No great company or building or work of art was ever created by accident. No World Series champion just lucked into the title. Sure, fortune (both good and bad) plays a part in all human endeavors. But there is no significant human achievement in any field—the arts, sports, business, politics or science—that did not start with a vision of what those involved wanted to accomplish. That vision, through thick and thin, in good times and bad, kept them moving forward together and helped them keep their eyes on the ultimate prize. Vision—a Noble Vision—of what we can accomplish together if we don't give in, give up or give out starts with leadership.

Help to Lead Your Family

Believe it or not, as the leader of your family, you are like Eisenhower in many ways. No, you are not fighting for the survival of the free world, but you are raising part of the next generation of that world. And, like Ike, that is the most important job you will ever have. Like Eisenhower, you must cast a powerful and positive vision of the future—a Noble Vision of your family's future.

To do that you must develop bonds of mutual respect and trust with your closest allies (your children's mother, your kids and your deepest friends). Like Ike, you must listen to them and understand their fears and frustrations. But you must also help them understand and buy into a shared Noble Family Vision and their role in making that vision a reality.

Also, like Ike, you will face great disappointment, discouragement and yes, even defeat. Sometimes it will seem that the wind and the tides are forever against you. At other times, your closest allies will deeply disappoint you. But if you keep on and see your Noble Vision for your family come to pass, you, your family, and our society—in fact, the entire world—will become the better for it.

Yes, it takes hard work, sacrifice and self-discipline. But it is the most important job you or I will ever have. Our personal future—and that of our children and their children—is at stake.

Building a Noble Vision for your family's future isn't something you do in a few minutes. But it is something you can start doing right now. Over time, I hope you will build a strong Noble Vision of what you want your family to be like. It is a big part—in fact, it is perhaps the most important part—of what I call a "Life Vision." A man's Life Vision will include three main things:

1. **Career Vision:** what you want to accomplish in your work life if you have the opportunity (which, in my opinion, our society tends to greatly overvalue).

2. **Personal Vision:** What type of man you want to be and be known as, what you want to be good at besides your work, and what you want people to say about you when you are gone.

3. **Noble Family Vision:** what your family will look like in 5 years, 10 years, 20 years. What you, as the leader of your family, are doing to build toward that goal.

The funny thing about the Noble Family Vision is that even though it is absolutely critical to a man's long-term happiness and fulfillment in life, it is not something most men spend much (or any) time thinking about, let alone planning for or actively working toward. That is understandable. In our culture today, if you can't make money selling it, you almost never hear about it. But, just like the other two elements of our Life Vision, if we as men don't think about it, plan for it and work toward it, nothing is going to happen.

Like each element of a man's Life Vision, the Noble Family Vision is going to require planning, work and sacrifice to bring it to pass. This is why it is so important for you to have the Noble Family Vision clearly in mind. There are so many competing priorities for dads today that it takes real discipline to keep your Noble Family Vision in balance and properly prioritized. In fact, it is such a challenge for so many dads today that the very first fatherhood tool we will look at is what I call the "Family First/Family Fun" tool (see Tool #1). This tool will help you make sure that your priorities and actions are the right ones in light of your Noble Family Vision. Trust me, seeing your Noble Family Vision come to pass will be worth all the hard work and sacrifice—times 10.

A Painful Personal Story

By the age of 50, I had accomplished a number of things that were somewhat unusual for a boy born in Toledo, Ohio, to a middle-class family that suffered from more than a few "generational curses." I wasn't unique or special in any way—I was of average height and weight and looks. And, unfortunately, my family wasn't much to brag about either: My dad was an alcoholic who changed jobs sometimes by the month. My mom did her best to keep us fed and clothed and out of harm's way. Our situation wasn't as bad as some families face, but it was not a good childhood.

By God's grace, a great education and a wonderful wife, by middle age I had been a Fulbright scholar to Asia, a Silicon Valley venture capitalist, a successful CEO, an international philanthropist, a senior U.S. diplomat and an Ivy League professor. Not bad for a pretty average kid from Toledo.

But I was also working way too hard—my family and I had moved too many times—and I was leaving my dear wife with far too much of the parenting responsibilities (note: teenage boys need their dads . . . period). As a result, I had put my own Family Vision at risk. A series of painful personal events brought this home to me. I had to make a choice, and I had to make it immediately. Was I going to get my Noble Family Vision back in balance with my Career Vision, or was it going to be second to my work? And, brother, please don't get me wrong here. We are not talking about what I was going to say—we are talking about what I was going to do. Wives and kids are very good at sniffing out hypocrisy. Saying that I would make the family a priority, and then continuing to devote 70-plus hours a week to my career and travelling 50 percent of the time wasn't going to cut it. I had to walk the talk.

That is where having a Noble Family Vision was so important. My wife and I could sit down and discuss where we wanted our family to be in the future, how we had gotten off track, and, most importantly, what we had to do to get back on track. It wasn't easy—and it wasn't always fun (especially for me). But it was important, and it helped draw us closer. I did make some big changes on the professional front—changes that gave me a lot more time with my family, which helped get my Life Vision back in balance. Yes, it did mean making some lifestyle changes—simplifying and cutting back in some areas. Was it the right decision? Absolutely! No question.

At the end of every chapter in this book you will find a set of questions titled "For Further Reflection." You can tackle these on your own, or you can use them as the basis for a good discussion with your family and/or your closest buddies. After the questions, you will find a set of "Today's Quick Wins." These are just for you—and they won't take you more than a few minutes to complete. They are designed to be a blessing to you.

Finally, at the end of this chapter, you will find a Put It to Work Guide. Every one of the Ten Tools listed in Part Two of this book also has a Put It to Work section at the end of the chapter. I hope you will find each of the Put It to Work Guides helpful, because if you're not putting the Ten Tools to work, you're probably not becoming a better dad. That would mean failure for both of us, and I hope you agree that when it comes to fatherhood, failure is not an option!

For Further Reflection

1. Do you think that building a Noble Family Vision for your family could help you and your entire family? Why or Why Not?

2. Do you agree that it is important to get your children's and their mother's buy-in for your Noble Family Vision? Why or why not?

3. How might a Noble Family Vision help you overcome some of the challenges you and your family face today? Tomorrow?

Today's Quick Wins

1. Take 60 seconds to envision what you want your family to look like, and be like, in 10 years.

2. Take 60 more seconds to immerse mind and heart in the strength and goodness of that vision.

3. Keep that vision in your "mental wallet" and bring it out to look at when things get tough.

Build a Noble Family Vision in the Next 10 Days

I hope you agree with me on the absolutely critical importance of your role as a father. It is the only job in the whole world that no one else can do better than you and it is the most important job you will ever have. Your future, your children's future and their children's future will be largely impacted by how well you do as a dad. That is why laying out a Noble Family Vision will help you and your family survive the storms of life together and thrive together. And, by the way, if you haven't experienced any storms yet—you must be a very young father! A shared Noble Family Vision can help each member of your family see the blessings of growing together and overcoming the storms of life as a strong and loving family team.

You, as the father of your family, have the pleasure and the responsibility of setting the tone and direction (along with your children's mother, of course) for your family's future. The reality is, if you don't do it, it probably won't get done. Just like a coach who forgets to give his team the plays for the big game, a father who doesn't help his family understand where they are going together—and why—is likely to be disappointed with the results.

Start Building Your Noble Family Vision Right Now

So let's take a few minutes—right now—to begin to develop a Noble Vision for your family. It's not hard; in fact, it is kind of fun. No matter where you are in your fatherhood journey, a Noble Vision for your family can help. If you are expecting your first child, this is a perfect time to sit down with your partner and make sure you both share a Vision for your family's future.

If your kids are almost off to college or work—even if they are already out of the nest—a Noble Family Vision can help you all share a common idea of what you want your larger family to look like in the future, including grandchildren. If you're a grandfather now, a Noble Family Vision for your extended family can help. Even if you are no longer married, you can still strive to have a positive and friendly relationship with your children's mother. It will greatly benefit your children, even though you may not be in their lives on a day-to-day basis.

So no matter where you are in life, and no matter how many disappointments you might have had as a dad, I encourage you to take a few minutes to really think about where you want your family to be in the future. Here are seven questions to help you build your Noble Family Vision. Answer these questions in the context of where you want to be in 5, 10, and 20 years:

1. What kind of relationship do you want to have with your children's mother? How do you want to interact and relate with her? If you are married, what do you want your marriage to look like? What do you hope she will say about you as a man, a husband and a father?

2. What kind of parent do you want to be? What do you want your children, when they are grown, to remember about your family life? How would you like them to characterize their childhood?

3. What do you want your kids to be like when they are adults? What do you want them to be known for . . . and known as?

4. How do you want your children to relate to their own spouses and children? What kind of husband or wife— and mom or dad—do you want your children to be?

5. How do you want your children to interact with each
   other in the future—and with each other's spouses and
   families?

6. How do you want your children to interact with you in
   the future? What kind of relationship do you hope to
   have with them?

7. What are the core values that help bind your family
   together? What do you all believe is truly important
   in life?

And There's Your Rough Draft!

Answering these seven questions will give you the basic outline of
your Noble Family Vision. And while you don't have to answer
each of these questions right now, I encourage you to grab a pen
and paper and write down as many answers as you can today. Just
get started. It won't take you long—and it is vitally important to
your future and your family's future.

Once you've gotten your answers written down, take a few
days to think about them, refine them and share them with your
family (if you feel comfortable doing that at this stage). Maybe
you might even want to discuss them with a close buddy or your
pastor/priest/rabbi. Over time, add the connecting phrases to
make your answers into a unified statement, instead of seven different answers. Little by little, you will be creating your own Noble Family Vision.

Don't worry that it's not perfect; of course it's not. But writing down a first draft, as rough as it might be, will get you halfway
there. There is a reason all great stories get recorded in books: the
written word lasts. Did you ever wonder why God gave the Ten
Commandments to Moses in written form? Because the written
word has staying power, and it has guiding power.

Trust me—it's not hard, but it is important. You don't have to
finish your Noble Family Vision in one go; instead, get a good first

draft and come back to it the next day and the next to finish it up. On page 44, you will see my family's Noble Vision, which I also hope is helpful. But please don't think yours has to be anything like ours—it does not. I'm just giving you one example. The important thing is to get started on your own, and then get it done.

Once you've got the beginning of your own Noble Family Vision written down, you're halfway home. But it has to be a Vision for your whole family, not just for you. So here's a suggestion: write a letter or email to your wife (or your children's mother) and get her thoughts, ideas and (eventually) her buy-in. A Noble Family Vision won't be as powerful without her full partnership in it, so be sure you're not trying to be a Lone Ranger dad. Get her input and buy-in from the start. (Again, if you don't have a wife—for whatever reason—don't panic. We will talk about being the best single dad you can be in Part Three of this book.)

Getting Your Wife's Input and Buy-in

The Bible is 100 percent correct when it teaches us that the man who has a good wife has received a true blessing from God. Yes, I know for those of us who are married, she's not perfect. But guess what? Neither are you or I . . . not by a long shot, brother! We will talk about the vital importance of loving our wives in Tool #2, "All-in Marriage," because that is one of the most important things a good father can do for his kids (not to mention his wife). In any event, it is very important to get your wife's input and buy-in for the Noble Family Vision.

To start the discussion on the right foot, tell her in advance that you'd like to talk with her about what kind of family you want to have in 5, 10, 20 years, and how you and she are going to get there. Ask her to think about her Family Vision in advance— give her the Family Vision questions listed above and the draft of your own Noble Family Vision (see, it does help to write it down). This will help her see how important this is to you. It will also help her to get her thoughts ready for a good discussion.

When the time comes, bring a pen and paper and write down her answers to those seven key questions and any other important ideas that come up. Ask her specifically what she thinks about each question and your answers. Find out where she agrees and what she might add or change. Listen closely (we guys are not always the best listeners) and ask lots of questions. Seek to deeply understand what she is saying, and why. I guarantee you will learn a lot about her, about yourself and about your family.

By the end of the discussion you will have a clear, shared Noble Family Vision. Or maybe it will take more discussion. That's fine. But be sure to include her suggestions and changes in your final draft of the Noble Family Vision, because in the end it has to be her Vision as well. By writing down the Vision and getting her agreement that what you've written accurately represents her thoughts, you will ensure that both of you share the same Noble Vision for your family, which is a very important first step.

Once you have a unified Noble Family Vision written down, it's time for a family meeting. If your kids are age 10 or younger, lay out the Vision for them in a way they can understand (you've got to make it age appropriate to be effective). But however you do it, be sure that each of your kids understands the Noble Vision that you and your children's mother have for the whole family. Discuss it with them, and see if they have any suggestions or changes. Make it abundantly clear that each child has an important role in making your Noble Family Vision a reality. If the kids have good ideas about how to make the Vision even stronger, be sure to incorporate them.

The results of the meeting might be surprising—or not. If you have teenagers, it probably won't be the easiest discussion (to be honest, that was the case for us). Regardless, laying out your Family Vision for your kids and asking for their help and buy-in will allow them to feel that they are part of the whole thing. If sharing and agreeing on the Family Vision is done with love and kindness and humor, it can even help draw you together as a family.

Once you've all agreed on your Noble Family Vision, finalize it in writing. If you can, have it written up nicely and framed (I am not kidding). Have it placed in a family area, such as in the kitchen or the family room, where everyone will see it frequently. At least twice a year (at the very minimum), ask your family, "How are we doing on our Noble Family Vision?" Be sure to keep the Vision in the forefront of everyone's mind. In other words, don't let it fade into the background.

With the passage of time, the Vision may require modification—or at least a new frame. But just its presence and the fact that you have set it out and explicitly made it a family priority will have big benefits down the road. It will help each member of your family better understand where you are going as a team—and where you want to end up.

A Noble Family Vision can be especially valuable in the tough times—and even the best families face tough times. It should also help you as a dad to see the importance of your role in leading your family toward this Noble Vision, for without effective leadership, even the most noble vision isn't much better than a dream. But with empowering servant leadership (which is Tool #5), families can stick together and persevere through even the toughest circumstances and see a beautiful future come to pass.

Here's the Noble Family Vision my wife and I developed for our family, which our kids (more or less) bought into. It's not perfect by a long shot (to be honest, some of our kids still have reservations about some of it), but for us it has been very helpful. I don't want you to think that your Noble Family Vision needs to be anything like ours. It does not. But I do want to share this with you to encourage you to complete your own Family Vision.

The Slayton Noble Family Vision

We are—and will strive to be—a family that serves the Lord, each other and our community for good. As we all grow up together we will do everything we can to preserve and to deepen the bonds between us, bonds of faith and love and joy. We will treat each other with kindness, always believing the best about each other. We will give each other the benefit of the doubt and will stick up for each other in thick or thin, no matter what.

As parents, we will put our children's and grandchildren's character, soul and future ahead of our own needs and desires. We will work hard for them and pray for them continually. May God help us be the very best Mother and Father we can be.

As the younger generation, we commit to living lives of integrity, courage and honor. We know that to do that will require God's help—so we will continue to seek His blessing and His guidance in all we do. We will seek to marry noble spouses who are strong in faith, rich in love and deep in wisdom. We will raise our own children in the love and wisdom of the Lord, as our Mom and Dad have tried their best to do for us. And we will do everything we can to strengthen and deepen the bonds of family down through the generations, no matter how many miles or time zones we might have to cross.

Once married, we the younger generation will not divorce our wives or husband. We will honor the example Christ set for us by talking out our differences, praying diligently for one another, and serving one another as Christ Himself served us. We will have a Noble Family Vision of our own—which will be in some ways different from this one. But in the most important elements we will do our best to pass on to our children that which the Lord passed on to us: the love and faith and joy and peace that comes from a happy family and the blessings of God Almighty.

In the years to come we will continue to honor our parents by caring for them as they cared for us when we were young.

They did not outsource us to nannies or boarding schools. We will not outsource them to old age homes or institutions . . . no matter what.

When tough times come, as they will, we will stick together and fight it out . . . together. We will go to the aid of any family member who needs help—anytime, anywhere. We will always be honest with each other, but in the love that Christ Himself has shown for each of us. And we will pray for one another and for each other's families. For we believe that "the diligent, effective prayer of the righteous is very, very powerful"—and we have seen that truth in our own home.

May the God of all Creation help bind our hearts together and bring this Noble Vision to pass, for His Greater Glory and the blessing of all Slaytons to come.

Amen.

3

Overview of the Ten Tools of Fatherhood

Like any skilled workman, a father needs a strong set of reliable tools to help him complete his job. These are the Ten Tools of Fatherhood—and they are effective in every home in which they are put to work.

If a man has even a small amount of skill, true dedication and a good family behind him, there's almost nothing he can't do.
ANONYMOUS

Mastering these 10 fatherhood tools has definitely made me a better husband, a better father and a better man.
JOHN M., SAN JOSE, CALIFORNIA

If you would like to discuss any of this material via email, feel free to contact me at **gws@beabetterdadtoday.com**

It's important to have a Noble Vision of where you are trying to lead your family. Just as important is making sure your children's mother shares that Vision. And getting your kids to buy in to the Vision with their inputs and ideas makes it even more powerful.

However, while a shared a Noble Family Vision is a powerful force for family good, by itself it is not enough. The goal, of course, is to build on your Noble Family Vision over time, with the right tools, and finally see it come to pass. That is the primary aim—seeing your Noble Family Vision come to pass—and it is one worthy of a man's life work.

I'm not saying it's easy, but with the right tools, dedication and help, you can do it. In fact, I *know* that it is possible. Yes, it will take hard work, but at least this is something that is truly worth working hard for. It will also take the right tools. In fact, it will take 10 specific sets of tools, which we are going to look at together in the following chapters. It will also take the help of family and friends who are on similar journeys. Just like the pioneers of the Old West experienced, no one successfully makes this journey alone. Finally, it takes God's grace, because each of us will make mistakes along the way. Trust me, I have made more than my share. But, as the Bible teaches us over and over again, His grace is sufficient for all who ask (see 2 Corinthians 12:9; Philippians 4:13).

I strongly believe that you have the basic skills and the desire to be an effective father. Otherwise, you would not be reading this book. And I hope that you are not too proud to ask God for His grace and guidance in becoming a better dad, because *all of us* need help to grow and mature and be the men He intended us to be. Each of us dads also needs to master the basic skills in the fatherhood toolset—the fundamental tools of fatherhood.

Take the 30-Day Challenge

This chapter will provide an overview of the Ten Tools of Fatherhood. In Part Two, we will look at each one of these tools in detail. Once you've read this chapter, you might want to go right to the specific tool you would like to work with first. That is fine. There is no reason you have to read the chapters in order or spend the same amount of time on each chapter.

As previously mentioned, you will find a Put It to Work Guide at the end of each chapter. The goal of the Put It to Work sections is to help you become a more skilled and confident father when using each of the Ten Tools.

Let me say right away that effective use of the tools is not going to happen overnight. Just like a small business owner, a skilled worker or a Major League baseball player, you can all improve your skill set no matter how long you have been doing your job. But it doesn't happen overnight. No one learns how to throw a good curve ball the first (or twentieth) time out. Just like any profession, being an effective dad has a basic skill set that takes time to master. But with practice, perseverance and partnership, you can master the Ten Tools of Fatherhood and become a (much) better dad.

I've seen these Ten Tools in use on every continent in the world. Certainly each culture has its own traditions and styles of parenting, but every great father I have ever met has mastered at least some of the basics of the Ten Tools. Different cultures may have different ways of expressing them, but the Ten Tools work in nearly every culture and place.

Let's look at them briefly now. As you examine these Ten Tools, notice that the first letter of each forms the easy-to-remember word F-A-T-H-E-R-H-O-O-D. This word can help you keep these tools in mind, even when you don't have this book in hand. These Ten Tools of Fatherhood will be effective in every home in which they are put to work, and I hope and pray that you will take the time to put each of them to work in your life and the life of your family.

Tool #1: Family First/Family Fun

When you enjoy the blessings of life with your family by putting them first today, you create a stronger family for tomorrow. Family fun time is the best time of all.

Fatherhood can be a lot of work, but it should also be a lot of fun. After all, you're on the journey of a lifetime (quite literally) with the people you most love in the whole world. Having fun with your family every day doesn't take lots of money or hours of free time. It just takes a willingness to enjoy the simple pleasures of life together and to celebrate the big things together as well. It also takes a conscious decision to put your family first each and every day.

Make no mistake, each of us decides what to put first in our lives. Some of us choose work, some of us chose worry, and some of us choose a hobby or our buddies, or a combination thereof. But by deciding to put our family first by wielding Tool #1 effectively, we not only enjoy today more but also build a stronger future for our family. That's because the good times we enjoy today create great memories for the future—memories that are like an invisible glue that binds a strong family together. Every family will face severe tests and challenges eventually. The father who uses Tool #1 today—and every day—will help his family to enjoy the moment and will strengthen his family for the unexpected storms of the future.

Tool #2: All-in Marriage

A committed marriage is the key to a happy family, which is why loving your wife is one of the greatest gifts you can give to your children (and your children's children).

Perhaps you have messed up as a father in the past. Even if that is true, there is hope for you in the future. You can repair some of the damage that has been done. The tools in this book, while they may seem unreachable at this point in your life, will provide you with some great goals toward which you can strive. With that in mind, let's go on.

The statistics could not be clearer: Kids who grow up in a generally happy home with both parents are at least twice as likely to have happy families themselves, go to college, hold down a long-term job, and be a productive member of society. Unfortunately, kids who don't have this kind of home-life are more than twice as likely to use drugs, have children out of wedlock, drop out of high school, be convicted of a felony, never hold a long-term job, suffer from severe psychological disorders, and die a violent death.[1] I know for sure that neither you nor I want that for our children.

Net-net: for your kid's sake, it is critical that you use Tool #2 to help build a happy and lasting marriage. That's not only important for your children—committed marriage is also extraordinarily important for your wife and for yourself. God designed marriage to be a place where you can be totally open, vulnerable and real with one other human being. For most of us, our marriage will be the only place in the world where we can learn to be exactly and fully who we are. But that is not easy—and it does not happen overnight. In fact, it will not happen without an all-in commitment from both husband and wife. If your wife doesn't know—or isn't sure—that you are truly for her and that you are going to be there for her in good times and bad, why would she open up the very depths of her heart to you? And make no mistake: as the leader of your family, it is up to you to demonstrate all-in commitment to your marriage. That is Tool #2, "All-in Marriage," which we will look at in Part Two of this book.

Of course, life is never as easy as we wish it were. If you are divorced or widowed, or you have had a child born outside of marriage, or if there are other reasons you are not living together as a family, let me first say thank you for your commitment to being a better dad despite a less-than-ideal situation. We will address these issues directly in the chapter titled, "Being the Best Single Dad You Can Be." I hope it will be a blessing to you, and I look forward to your ideas and input on how to strengthen the chapter.

Tool #3: True Moral Compass and True Humility

Setting a high moral standard for yourself and your family—and transferring those standards to your children over time—is the most important inheritance you as a father can give to your children.

Many people think long and hard about the material things they will pass on to their kids when they die. In fact, there is a large estate planning industry in the United States and around the world that does nothing but help parents with inheritance planning of the material kind.

But there is something much more important that we as fathers need to pass on to our children: a strong set of ethics and time-tested values, or what I call a "True Moral Compass." This is the most important legacy we can ever give our kids. A True Moral Compass will serve them well in both good times and bad, even after we are long gone. I realize that talking about a True Moral Compass goes against the grain of much of our culture today, where so few people want to even talk about enduring moral and ethical values. But the Moral Compass Tool is essential to who we are as men, and it will be essential for our children if we want them to live lives of courage, character and commitment.

Of course, before you can pass on a True Moral Compass to your children, you have to be sure that your own Moral Compass is working properly. If it is not, with God's help you must fix it. Then and only then will you be in a position to pass it on to your kids. It is the greatest gift you can give to your children, because how else will they guide themselves in this world if their own Moral Compass isn't working? The truth is simple: If they don't learn it from you, they are unlikely to ever learn it at all.

Tool #4: Heartfelt Love

It is through commitment, fidelity, grace and tenderness that you show your family—in word and in deed—how much you love them (and therefore how valuable they are to you . . . and to God).

I know this one sounds basic, and it is. But love is the basis on which a strong family foundation is built. I'm not talking about the sappy, puppy dog love of seventh grade. I'm talking about the 'til death do us part, real world we're-going-to-make-it-through-this-together type of love that determines whether a family makes it or not. If you've been married more than a year, you know that the sparkle and romance of the honeymoon wears off. But if you work at it, sparkle and romance is replaced over time by things much stronger and durable: mutual respect, interdependence, a relationship in which each member is mutually dependent on the other, and the joy of intimately knowing and being known.

Developing the skill to love the members of your family—in ways each one can understand and appreciate—is one of the most important fatherhood tools you need to develop. And trust me, just like hitting a baseball or catching a football, all of us can get better at this skill.

Tool #5: Empowering Servant Leadership

Empowering your family by putting their needs above your own will yield rich benefits today . . . and for generations to come. This is the essence of great fatherhood.

Service before self is the essence of all great leadership. It requires our willingness to put our family's needs and wants above our own. And it is not easy. Most of us are pretty good at taking care of our own wants and needs. Western society today would have us believe that taking care of our own needs, "looking out for #1," is the essential job of every man. But that is *not* true. In fact, it cannot be true for you if you really want to be an effective father.

Twenty centuries ago, the apostle Paul encouraged all men to love their wives (and family) "as Christ loved the church . . . and gave Himself for her" (Ephesians 5:25). That advice has certainly stood the test of time. Servant leadership is not only good for our families but also good for us as well, for in serving them effectively, we become stronger and better men ourselves.

Tool #6: Relationship Tools that Work

To be good a dad, you also need the willingness to listen, the skill to truly hear, and the ability to relate deeply with your family.

Let's face it, guys: most of us are not the world's best listeners. Most of us are action-oriented instead of feelings-oriented. That's not a bad thing. But a family, at its essence, is about relationships. We must be able to truly hear and understand each member of our family if we are to build a lifelong relationship with them. This is where many of us dads get into trouble. How many times have I heard these words from men whose families have gone over the proverbial cliff: "I gave them everything they needed. I provided for them financially. Where did I go wrong?"

The truth is that we must provide for our family, but, as we will examine in Tool #10, "Dynamic, Whole-Person Support," we must also provide for them emotionally, mentally, physically and spiritually. The only way to be an effective emotional, mental and spiritual provider is to develop a real relationship with each member of your family—and that starts with listening and understanding them.

The Relationship Tool is basic to many of the others, and it is a natural outgrowth of Tool #4, "Heartfelt Love." Each one of us can improve our listening and relationship skills. Not only are they critical tools for us as fathers, but they can also help us develop more productive and positive friendships and business relationships outside the family as well.

Tool #7: Heaven's Help

To be the best earthly father you can be, you need help from the Ultimate Father.

No matter what your take is on spiritual matters, I hope you can agree that we as dads need as much help as we can get. If God truly is our heavenly Father, and He loves you and me as His sons (as Jesus taught), doesn't it follow that He wants to help you to be the very best earthly father you can be? Given this, doesn't it make sense to ask Him for help?

Many years ago when I was an agnostic, a dear friend of mine challenged me to ask God to reveal Himself to me. I did—and He did. Over time, and with many bumps in the road, it changed my life completely . . . and all for the better. We all need a rich source of love and joy and wisdom and peace in our lives. That is especially true of moms and dads, because our children look to us for those assets all the time. If God's love and joy and wisdom and peace are available to every single one of us who ask Him to reveal Himself to us and believe in Him, as the Bible clearly teaches, we'd be foolish not to ask for His help.

Tool #8: Other Good Dads

*There are no successful Lone Ranger dads—
you need the support of friends and older role models
from whom you can learn.*

It is impossible for us to be successful dads on our own. We are, by nature, social beings. Yes, we may not have as big a need for social interaction as women do, but the need is still there. If we fulfill that need by hanging around with guys who are chasing skirts or who clearly don't care too much about their families, that is going to rub off on us. We can't kid ourselves—bad friends trump good intentions. That's just the way it is for most of us. On the other hand, if we consciously seek out men of character, commitment and competence who care deeply about their families, we will be influenced for the better.

The positive influence of other good dads, and especially those who can be good role models for us, is very powerful. That's why good fathers in cultures the world over have close friends who themselves are committed to their families . . . and to their friends. We need the help of other good men of strong character—and they need ours. This tool will show how to find and build those positive and productive friendships with like-minded men who also desire to be good fathers.

Tool #9: Optimistic, Never-Surrender Attitude

*No matter how tough things get, you can never, ever, quit on your
family. Winning dads never quit, and dads who quit never win.*

This is one of the most important tools for every effective father— and one that each of us needs to develop. We may be able to do a great job with the other nine tools, but if we don't have practice using this one, all our work could be for naught.

It reminds me of one of the best lessons I learned at Harvard, where I did my MBA. There was a well-researched study of successful CEOs and their less-successful peers. The study determined that there was one primary difference that existed across all industries and all cultures. Every single executive in the study—and that included scores of senior executives from companies around the world—had endured painful and potentially career-ending professional and/or personal setbacks. Failed projects, disastrous acquisitions, missed promotions and even outright demotions—each CEO had experienced significant professional failure. But the successful ones were those who made the conscious decision to fight through their failures, to learn from them and not give up. Likewise, we as dads have to learn to fight through the setbacks, both big and small, that inevitably come to all families.

Developing the inner strength and moral courage to never give up on your family as a whole—that is a man's man. And that's what this tool is all about.

Tool #10: Dynamic, Whole-Person Support

It is critically important for you to support your family emotionally, physically, mentally and spiritually—not just financially.

Notice that "financially" came last. That is because so many of us (including myself for too many years) over-emphasize its importance. In fact, at least for me, being a good provider justified a lot of behavior on my part that really was not good for my family at all: working too late, being away from home too much, moving my family too frequently and being overly devoted to my job.

Yes, we have to provide materially for our families, sometimes in conjunction with our working spouse. But providing for them emotionally, physically, mentally and spiritually is just as important. If you're too tired from your efforts at work to provide those other things, you probably need to make some changes.

The next section of this book, Part Two, has a specific chapter devoted to each of these Ten Tools of Fatherhood, the basic elements of the Fatherhood Toolset. We are going to look at a number of ways to help expand and sharpen our skills in each of these key areas. And don't neglect the Put It to Work Guide that accompanies each of these chapters. To paraphrase a video game hero my sons like to quote, "It's GROW time, baby!"

For Further Reflection

1. Which of the Ten Tools might be most important for your family? Why?

2. Which of the Ten Tools are you strongest in, and which do you need to improve? Do your wife (or children's mother) and your children agree?

3. Can you think of any critical fatherhood tools that I've neglected? (If so, let me know at www.facebook.com/BeaBetter DadToday.)

Today's Quick Wins

1. Take 60 seconds to think about the last time you used one of the Ten Tools well with your family.

2. Take 60 more seconds to reflect on how good that felt and how good it was for both them and you.

3. Take 60 seconds to envision having those kinds of moments with each member of your family every day, and how much stronger that would make your relationships.

Note
1. *Father Facts,* fifth edition, National Fatherhood Initiative, 2007. http://www.father hood.org/organizations/programs/father.

PART TWO

The Ten Tools of Fatherhood

TOOL #1

Family First/Family Fun

When you enjoy the blessings of life with your family by putting them first today, you create a stronger family for tomorrow. Family fun time is the best time of all.

Do not be deceived . . . a man reaps what he sows.
GALATIANS 6:7, *NIV*

Early in my career, I thought to myself, "What am I working for everyday?" The answer was "my family and their welfare." So I made a pact early with myself that I would put family first. This meant crafting my own career so that I would not be traveling a lot, finding ways to plan out my week so I could be home for dinner with my family and cutting out weekend work when the kids were young. Not easy to do, but 20 years later I know I made the right decision.

RANDY H., PLEASANTON, CALIFORNIA

If you would like to discuss any of this material via email, feel free to contact me at **gws@beabetterdadtoday.com**

You might think, *Wow, this first tool is a no-brainer. I'm good at that already.* Maybe you are. Maybe. But I've found that many dads have lost the ability to put their families first and have fun with them. Of course, very few of us would ever admit this. But here is a simple test: Do you have fun with your family *on a frequent, regular basis,* or did you when you had the opportunity?

If your answer is "not too often" or "I'm not sure" or "you don't understand my situation," read on. Even if your answer is "sometimes," you probably could strengthen your use of this tool. In fact, *all* of us could strengthen our skill with this tool.

For too many of us, weeks, months and even years go by, and there's too much strain, stress and striving and too little laughter, love, lighthearted fun or quality time of any type with dad. That is really tough on our families—and especially on our children. Why does this happen? I believe that in many cases we as dads choose, consciously or unconsciously, to put something (or multiple things) in front of our family. We all choose what we focus on in life, and if we choose to put work or worry or our bank account or something else in front of our families, we will eventually reap what we sow.

Do you know how most children spell the word "love"? T-I-M-E. And fun time as a family is the best T-I-M-E of all. Fun time doesn't have to be a grand vacation (although good family vacations are great). It can just be time rolling around with your kids on the floor when you are with them, watching a good movie together, or teaching a child a new skill you have learned. It can even be helping your son or daughter with their homework—as long as it's done in the right way.

Fun family time can be almost anything that gets your family out of the normal routine and focused on each other. Not only will you have fun together (and that's one of the best things about family life) but you'll also be creating warm and wonderful memories.

These memories you create will have a dual purpose. First, they will help you and each member of your family know that he or she is special . . . and specially loved. Second, over time, good memories are like cement for a well-constructed wall. They will help your family hang together when the storms of life threaten to knock you down or break you up . . . and those storms come to all of us. And if the storms have already knocked down your wall, it's time to start building again. You can do it.

Don't worry if you're a "long-distance dad"—you can still put your family first and have fun with them on a consistent basis. In fact, we have a whole chapter in Part Three devoted to long-distance dads. Feel free to turn to that section right now if you are living far from your family. Because no matter how far you are from your family physically, they need your love, support and encouragement in their lives.

One father, a senior executive at a large U.S. company, told me, "It came down to this: Was I going to put my family first and save it, or was I going to put my career first and have a shot at becoming CEO? Well, I'm now a divorced CEO . . . and I will always regret that." Let's learn from his mistake.

These days you have with your family really are, right now, "the good old days." Wherever you are in life and whatever the age of your kids (or grandkids), in 10 or 20 years you will look back on this time with one of two primary emotions: you will either regret that you did not have fun with your children (or grandchildren), or you will be thankful for all the fun times you had together. Or maybe, if you're like most men, you will have both emotions—and both will be justified. But one thought I guarantee you will not have: *I should have spent more time pursuing my own interests.*

A Few Ideas to Promote Family Fun

This is why it is vital for you to develop what I call the "Family First/Family Fun Tool." This is a hugely useful tool and one that you should use as much as possible. You don't need lots of money, or fancy vacations, or really much of anything material. You just need the willingness to give quality time and attention to your family—and sometimes you need a little imagination to do things that are new, different and, yes . . . fun.

So how do we as dads develop our Family First/Family Fun Tool? We'll go into that in detail in the Put It to Work Guide that follows this chapter, but here are some ideas from some excellent fathers I've seen who are doing a great job with this tool in very different parts of the world. I hope some of them will give you some good ideas (and please be sure to share with us all your creative family fun ideas at www.facebook.com/BeaBetterDadToday).

Ken, in Northern California, taught me the importance of learning to like whatever my kids liked to do. "Now, I will be the first to admit that I am not into video games," Ken says. "And I think that many, if not most, American teenage boys spend WAY too much time in front of screens of all types. So we should all try to limit our sons' video gaming and Facebooking (which requires real effort, by the way). But from time to time, I will hang out with my boys and watch them play *Call of Duty*, or whatever. I might even try my hand at it—which is always good for a laugh, as I am without question the worst *Call of Duty* player ever. But we laugh, we have fun . . . and we talk. And for that, I'll play almost anything."

My buddy John in Seattle showed me the importance of having fun with other dads and their boys. "In our rush-rush Western culture," John says, "more of us dads need to spend time with friends who have kids our age. Playing baseball together or building a flagpole or a multi-family hike on the beach . . . these are all fun for everyone. Your kids will build deeper friendships, and they will also watch (and learn from) how you interact with your friend(s)." Good stuff.

"Uncle Pete" in Maryland taught me the importance of setting a consistent time to be with my kids. In spite of a challenging day-to-day schedule, Pete makes sure to have a monthly adventure with his young son. Sometimes it's as simple as a bike ride on the Potomac, going to Home Depot for their kids' workshop, or flying kites at the annual kite flying festival on the Mall. Once it was a trip to Florida to see the space shuttle launch. The important thing is that it's a regular part of his and his family's life. It's a priority. And it is fun. Through these times together, Pete is building the bonds of a great father/son relationship, showing his son how special and important he is, and teaching him how to deal with the planned and unplanned adventures that real life brings.

My friend Randy on the West Coast taught me the importance of establishing regular "fun routines" with my kids. Every weekend he and his family would take a walk, and most weekends they would watch a family movie together. These became priceless memories over time—not of one particular walk or a certain movie, but a hybrid of different walks and different movies and the conversations they created that blended together into a beautiful picture.

Our dear friends Emilio and Valeria have always taken their kids out to dinner with them. They own some great restaurants, so getting their kids involved early was good for the whole family. It helped their children to develop excellent manners and to learn how to conduct conversations with all types of people—plus they always had a lot of fun. Some of the best dinners our family has ever had have been with them. Our kids loved them. Their kids loved them. And we adults loved them. Even though we live in different countries now, we still try to have dinner together at least once a year. Wonderful times—and wonderful memories.

The Importance of Putting Family First

"There was a long time in my life when I wondered if I'd ever be a father," says Bruce, from Chicago. "I didn't get married until I was 36, and I didn't have my first child until 40. At the age of 52, I now have three sons, 12, 9 and 4. Being an older dad compared to most, I now realize why most people choose to become parents sooner . . . when they have more energy! I have learned over the years, however, that wisdom and willingness to love and serve are much more important than energy in raising children. As fathers, we all have a conscious choice each day to focus the best of our time and resources on our relationships with our spouse and children or let that time slip away in extra work hours, hobbies, TV shows, watching sports, house projects, and various other non-family centered activities.

"Early on, I resolved to be a 'hands on' dad even if it meant doing activities where I didn't have much aptitude or skill. To make time for this, I decided to limit certain personal activities like golf, personal exercise and reading—all of which are good things. I also made a commitment to limit my work travel and evenings out so I could spend time in the evenings with my family.

"Now, after many years of coaching various youth sports (where I have little talent), being an assistant scoutmaster for a Boy Scout troop, spending untold hours assisting in Lego projects, and playing children's games, I have come to see that the 'personal sacrifices' I made really weren't sacrifices at all. In fact, I now truly 'count it all joy' to have had so many memorable moments with my sons."

Mohamed, in West Africa, taught me the importance of teaching my kids to love something that I love. The secret is to bring them along with you whenever you can and allow them to participate more and more over time. Maybe it's fishing or tennis or building model airplanes or star gazing . . . or tracking wildebeest on the Savannah. It doesn't matter. If you love to do it—and if it's appropriate for the kids—bring them. Maybe not every time, but as often as you can. They will grow to love whatever you're doing together, just because it represents a special time with dad. And, over time, they will grow to be quite good at it too. Eventually, they will be teaching you a thing or two . . . and what could be better than that?

Anyway, you get the picture. You can do it. There are (almost) no bad ideas for fun with your family. Just do something to interact with your kids. If it's really different and creative—and if it goes well—let us all know about it at www.facebook.com/BeaBetter DadToday. You will be helping all of us.

If you put your family first—and take time to have fun with your kids—you'll build a stronger family now and in the days to come. As the Bible tells us about the importance of holidays and good family memories: "These days were to be remembered and celebrated throughout every generation" (Esther 9:28, *NASB*). So let's do that. Let's put our families first. And let's celebrate and have fun with our families whenever we have the chance. Doing so will make life's journey all the sweeter.

For Further Reflection

1. If you are married, do you try to have fun with your wife and kids on a regular basis? How would your wife and kids answer that question?

2. What could you do to further enhance the joy in your family?

3. What kind of changes do you need to make to free up more family fun time?

Today's Quick Wins

1. Take 60 seconds to remember a great fun time you had with your family—and think about what made it so much fun.

2. Take 60 seconds to reflect on how good it felt to laugh and have fun with your family, both for you and for them. Meditate on how good it was to be together like that.

3. Take 60 seconds to think of another fun activity that you can do with your kids. Then do it.

Put It to Work Guide

Your Family First/
Family Fun Toolset

Here's a challenge that will help you to dramatically sharpen your Family First/Family Fun Tool. Commit yourself to doing something fun with your kids during the next 30 days. Try to make having fun together a "habit" of sorts—something you and the kids look forward to during that time.

When you are able to contact your family, plan something fun for them. Again, please do not worry if you are a long-distance dad or if you do not live near your family. Your Family First/Family Fun Tool is still important—and you can still use it actively. It's just going to take a little more work and creativity. If you want to do so, turn to the chapter in Part Three on long-distance dads for 30 ideas on how to put your Family First/ Family Fun Tool to work.

If your kids are a bit older, you will have to plan your family fun times a bit more. Maybe you can watch the same ball game and later discuss it. You could plan a backpack trip together, or how you will climb a mountain or learn a new sport or skill. Anticipation is half the fun. If your older kids are good at something specific (and I am sure they are), help them develop their skills in that area. You don't have to be as good as they are at soccer or movie making or debate or playing the drums. You can still encourage them and help them develop their own special skills.

We're going to be looking at the benefits of a good marriage in the next chapter. Whether your marriage is a good one or not, I'm sure you want your children to have good marriages. You know the old saying, "happy wife; happy life." There is a lot to that saying, brother, and we need to keep it in mind. So read on and pass what you are learning on to your children. Be open to talking to them about any mistakes you have made in your life and what you would do differently if you had the opportunity.

Take the 30-Day Challenge

I want to challenge you to doing something fun with every member of your family at least once during the next 30 days. This could be something as simple as playing a game together or just sharing some stories. Regardless of what you do, the idea is to just spend time together. You'll be happy with the results, and I'm sure your family will be happy as well. Again, that doesn't mean spending hours and hours each day; it just means devoting 10 minutes of your time to the interests and needs of your children. The secret, of course, is to keep going beyond the 30 days. Go to 60 days, and begin to make it a good habit. Stretch to 90 and then 180 days. You will soon begin to see the positive fruit of your Family First/ Family Fun Tool. Once you get to a full year, you will have strengthened your Family First/Family Fun Tool considerably, and your family will be all the stronger for it.

Let's Put Our Excuses Aside

Maybe you're saying to yourself, *I'm too tired at the end of the day,* or *I'm too far away to do that,* or *I have too many other responsibilities.* These may be real issues, but to each of them I have one simple response: Rubbish. You can do it—IF you make it the priority it should be. At the end of the day, what's more important? Again, if you are a single dad living away from your children, this 30-day practice session is more difficult to implement, but the basic idea is still the same: make the most of whatever time you have with your kids. Even if you are divorced or otherwise single, your kids need you. Remember that excuses are just that . . . excuses.

Life needs to be fun . . . as much of the time as possible. This is one of the greatest blessings of having a good family. Even if you've had the worst day (and trust me, I've had my share), you can be encouraged and revitalized by your family. You can't always be toiling away, worrying about the bills or your particular circumstances or something that might never happen. As Jesus teaches us, worry is completely useless (see Matthew 6:25-34). Most worries never come to pass, and worrying about things never changes anything anyway. Better to enjoy today to its fullest with your family and dearest friends. Let tomorrow's worries take care of themselves.

So make plans to do something special with one—or all—of your family. The ability to put your family members first and have fun with them is a vital tool in your fatherhood skill set. It really isn't hard—in fact, it truly is fun. Don't get discouraged if your plans fall through here or there—that's not the point. The goal is to get in the habit of having fun with your family every time that you can—for the rest of your lives. It's worth it. So let's get started!

A Heartbreaking Story of Father Absence

I remember a young man who was (and is) a good friend of one of our sons. His mom and dad were divorced, and his dad lived four to five hours away. His dad rarely made time for his son—and this has had a very negative impact on the young man. One day when this young man was at our house, he told us how excited he was that his dad was driving up to celebrate Christmas with him that coming weekend (it was mid-January, but the dad had not made time to see his son in December). Later that same night, he got a text from his dad telling him he couldn't make it. The look of anguish, of abandonment, of despair on that young man's face was something I will never forget. I have no idea what the "dad" was doing that weekend, but I guarantee you it wasn't worth the pain and damage he inflicted on his son.

TOOL #2

All-in Marriage

*A committed marriage is the key to a
happy family, which is why loving your wife is one
of the greatest gifts you can give to your children
(and your children's children).*

---

*Husbands, love your wives, as Christ loved the
church and gave himself up for her.*
EPHESIANS 5:25, *ESV*

*Learning how to be an "all-in" husband and father has brought
stability and a peace to our family that I honestly did not think possible.
But it did. And I am a much better man for it.*
PETER M., WASHINGTON, DC

If you would like to discuss any of this material via email,
feel free to contact me at **gws@beabetterdadtoday.com**

The impact of divorce and a father's absence on children is devastating. You won't read about it in the *New York Times,* but the statistics are overwhelmingly clear. Children from homes where the mom and dad are in a committed marriage, when compared to those who are not, are more than twice as likely to graduate from high school or college, hold down a steady job in adulthood, have a successful marriage themselves and live to a ripe old age.[1] Children from broken homes are more than twice as likely to do drugs, go to jail, drop out of high school, suffer from mental illness, fail to hold down any job for more than a year, have babies out of wedlock, and die an early death than their more fortunate peers.[2]

It's no exaggeration to say that America is now being divided into two groups with huge disparities between the two in virtually every meaningful measure of happiness, contentment or social productivity. And the line that divides these two groups is not racial, ethnic, financial or linguistic; the line is their parental background.

Which group do you want your kids to be in?

I'm sure you want the very best for your children. So let me just lay it out for you: If you are married, one of the most important gifts you can give your children is to love your wife and be faithful to her. That's what an All-in Marriage is all about. And that's what I believe 99 percent of wives are looking for from their husbands.

Hopefully you have a good wife who loves you and your children. If you do, don't take her for granted. God's Word tells us that a good wife is far more valuable than the most precious rubies or jewels (see Proverbs 31:10). That is most certainly true. Ask almost any dad who has lost his wife early in life. He will tell you. That old Joni Mitchell song is too often right: "You don't know what you've got 'til it's gone."

Your spouse is probably the only person in the world who loves your kids even more than you do. That's the way most moms are wired. That's why a courageous mom in rural India will face down a tiger instead of give up her child. That's why a courageous mom in Los Angeles will crash through walls of government paperwork to get her autistic boy the help he needs. That is one of the greatest things in the world about moms. And if they see that we dads are committed to them and to our children, they will be our biggest allies. We need their help, not only for raising our children but also for growing ourselves into the fullness of manhood.

The Mirror of Marriage

Marriage is frequently difficult and discouraging. Why is that? I believe it is because we are all, every single one of us, deeply flawed human beings. And our flaws tend to grow over time unless we recognize them, understand them and correct them. That is one of the many reasons that it is not good for "man to be alone" (Genesis 2:18, *NASB*).

I remember when I was about to get married. An older friend asked me if I thought I was fundamentally selfish. Being the young pup that I was, I said no. And I really felt deep down that I wasn't; after all, I had just spent five years of my life serving the poor in Asia and Africa. Over the years, I've reflected on that statement and my own lack of self-awareness many times, because the truth is that I was quite selfish. I just didn't know it.

A good marriage serves many purposes; one of them is to hold up a mirror to each other's soul. If you let her, your wife can help adjust and focus that mirror, emphasizing your strengths while helping you understand your weaknesses. You might not like seeing them, but you need to do so. Like a stain on the back of my suit jacket, no one but my wife is going to tell me about it. A good wife also realizes that behind all the male bravado some of us guys exhibit, most of us have real fears and uncertainties about ourselves. A good wife can help her husband not only understand and correct his weaknesses but also bring external validation to the strengths that make him who he is. We can and should serve our wives (very gently, of course) in the same way.

This is one of the most beautiful (though at times difficult) things that happens in a good marriage. My wife can help me truly see myself more accurately. Over time, just as "iron sharpens iron," my wife has helped me shore up parts of my character that were seriously out of whack (things that, to be honest, I didn't even see in myself before we were married). She has also helped me recognize and build upon strengths that I didn't know I had. In doing this, by God's grace, she has helped me to become a much better man.

The 50 Percent Rule

No wife is perfect, no more than any man is perfect. Yet when I hear some guys talk, it seems that they are expecting near perfection in their wives. Can I just say something to all us guys who have been married more than a few years . . . and who might be disappointed in some ways with our wives? I want to commend to your attention what I call "The 50 Percent Rule." Think about that in the context of baseball. No one in the history of Major League Baseball has ever hit .500, or even close. And let's face it, Dad, you and I are lucky—very lucky—if we match up to 50 percent of the vision that our wives had for us when we married. That's the way human expectations are versus reality.

So if your wife is even 50 percent of what you had hoped for when you married, count yourself blessed. And if you begin to wield your All-in Marriage Tool effectively, no matter how far away you are, I bet you will see a marked improvement in that number. The point here is that you and I both need the committed help of our wives to be the best dads we can be. This isn't just true sometimes in some cultures. This is true at all times and across all cultures.

What about if you and your wife are having serious problems in your marriage? Brother, all I can say is this: You are not alone. In fact, research shows that the majority of marriages go through periods of significant challenges where one or both partners think about separation or divorce.[3] So what makes the difference between those marriages that end up on the rocks of divorce and those that survive the tough times to grow stronger and even more committed? That's a big question—and I hope to devote an entire book to the issue of building a great marriage one day soon. But this is not that book. So instead, let me just offer a few suggestions that have proven their power in many marriages over the years.

Stop the Comparisons

First, get rid of any and all competitors to your wife. Let's not kid ourselves. This is one of the root causes of dissatisfaction and/or disillusionment in many marriages today. You might fantasize about a woman you have met—or it might be an image of the "perfect woman" you hold on to in your mind. It might be a question that comes to you in tough times: "What would have happened if I had married Sally?" Or it might be the unhealthy and unrealistic garbage that is so prevalent on the Internet. Whatever it is, get rid of it.

None of these women will ever be the mother of your children. None will have devoted the best years of her life to helping you become the man you are today. None will have shared the joys and heartaches of raising a family with you. And the statistics are very clear: None of the comparisons is at all likely to be a better wife to you. The divorce rate for second marriages is almost twice that of first marriages. Yes, there's a reason God's Word instructs us to be satisfied with the wife of our youth (see Proverbs 5:18). We will talk more about this in Tool #9, "Optimistic, Never-Surrender Attitude," but you must "burn the other boats" if you want to successfully focus on making your marriage and your family successful. You must put out of your mind any and all competitors to your wife, whether real, digital or imaginary.

Why is that? First of all, that is the only way to be fair to your wife. You see your wife at her best . . . and at her worst. How frequently do you see other women in their curlers . . . or feeling sick . . . or mad because you forgot to pick something up at the store? Answer: never. Is that because other women do not wear curlers or get sick or get mad? No, it's simply because you do not live with them day in and day out.

Second, you made a vow before God and before your closest and dearest friends to honor and cherish your wife "in sickness and in health." I am not exaggerating when I say that our society is founded upon that vow. In honoring it, we not only honor our wives and bless our children but also strengthen the society and the nation in which we live.

Third, you owe it to your wife. Don't think for a second that there aren't guys out there who are more handsome, more charming and more successful than you are. Do you want your wife to be fantasizing about them? Obviously not. So let us each be the leader we need to be in this area and get rid of any competitors (imaginary or otherwise) to our wives.

Divorce Is Not an Option

We also need to put the idea of divorce completely out of the picture. In fact, we shouldn't even consider divorce as an "option." Some men seem to think that if they could just marry someone other than their wife—like that cute woman who works nearby or that beautiful movie star they see on the screen—they'd be happy. But the facts tell us otherwise. Again, the statistics are crystal clear on this: Second marriages fail at almost twice the rate of first marriages. The problems that destroyed the first marriage are frequently the same problems that destroy the second marriage. Divorce isn't a way to deal with problems; frequently it is just a way to avoid the hard work of personal change. If we don't deal with our own issues, they pop up again, sometimes worse than before. And while the impact of divorce on adults is usually quite negative, its impact on the children involved is almost always truly devastating.

Where the Green Grass Grows

Take every opportunity, every day, to build up your marriage and your family. Yes, the grass really is greener where you water it—so let's be sure to water our own marriage and family. We will look at three different ways to build an All-in Marriage in the Put It to Work Guide at the end of this chapter. You don't have to use each of these ideas (actually, you don't have to use any of them), but you do have to take the lead in building a good marriage and a happy family. These three proven tools should help you be a better all-in husband and father, which will lead directly to a stronger marriage and family.

An All-Too-Common Divorce Story

My neighbor Robert (not his real name) believed that divorcing his wife would make his life better. No more hassles and no more "unreasonable" demands on his time . . . or at least that's what he thought. So when a lonely female colleague suggested they have dinner together, he did not resist. From there the marriage went downhill quickly. Adultery has a way of doing that. He sued for divorce. His wife and his kids pleaded with him to try to work things out, but he was adamant. He thought things would just be so much better for him when the divorce came through.

However, there were a few things my neighbor forgot about. He was shocked when his wife got half the assets . . . plus the house. He was saddled with significant alimony payments, which he was legally bound to make. Worst of all for him, he could now only see his kids twice a month—and they blamed him for the divorce. And guess what? That lonely female colleague turned out to be a lot more demanding than his ex-wife. Robert has had more hassles and demands on his time from her than he ever had from his wife and kids.

So, brother, let us learn from that good, old expression about the grass always being greener on the other side of the fence. The truth is that it's always greener where you water it.

The reality is that as the leader of your household, you hold the primary responsibility for the success or failure of your marriage. Yes, it takes the enduring commitment of both husband and wife to make a good marriage, just as it takes two to tango. But just as in dancing, someone must take the lead. By nature and by nurture, in societies and cultures around the world, that responsibility falls to us as men. The good news is that in shouldering that responsibility, we become stronger men ourselves.

Rich or poor, black or white, Hispanic or Asian, college graduate or high school diploma, at the end of the day, each of us has to look at himself in the mirror and ask the fundamental question: "What kind of man am I, and what kind of man do I want to be?" Be an "All-in Marriage" man. Mark Twain had it right when he said, "No man or woman really knows what perfect love is until they have been married a quarter of a century."

For Dads Who Aren't Married

What do you do if you don't have a wife? That is a fair question. It's also a very big question, given the astronomical divorce rate in the U.S. these days. The answer differs depending on the context of the question—and there is no easy answer. For this reason, I've devoted a full chapter to the issue of single-parenting in Part Three of this book. Being a single dad is far from an optimal situation, and I salute those single dads who desire to be the best fathers possible for their kids. It is still the most important job you will ever have. So, if you're a single dad, please feel free to go right to the chapter in Part Three titled "Being the Best Single Dad You Can Be" and check it out now.

If you're a married man, thank God for your wife right now and ask Him to help make you an "All-in Marriage" man today. It's the best gift you can ever give to your wife, your kids and yourself.

Finally, do check out the Put It to Work Guide at the end of this chapter. As with every Put It to Work Guide, this one has specific suggestions, ideas and action plans for you to strengthen your All-in Marriage Tool. I look forward to getting your feedback, suggestions and ideas at www.facebook.com/BeaBetterDadToday.

For Further Reflection

1. Do you have an All-in Marriage from your side? From your wife's side?

2. If yes, what can you do to further strengthen your marriage? If no, what are the biggest obstacles to creating an All-in Marriage for you? For your wife?

3. Do you (and she) have the courage to face these obstacles head-on . . . and overcome them?

Today's Quick Wins

1. Take 60 seconds to think back to your wedding day, and meditate on all the best parts of it.

2. Take 60 seconds to reflect on the three or four things you most loved about your wife when you married her, and remember that they are still within her.

3. Take five minutes to do something nice for your wife right now. Write her a "Love You" card or email, invite her out on a date, do the dishes for her, go pick her (or buy her) some flowers. But do it today . . . for sure.

Further Reading

Timothy Keller with Kathy Keller, *The Meaning of Marriage: Facing the Complexities of Commitment with the Wisdom of God* (New York: Dutton, 2011).

Barry and Lori Byrne, *Love After Marriage* (Ventura, CA: Regal, 2012).

Dr. H. Norman Wright, *Bringing Out the Best in Your Wife* (Ventura, CA: Regal, 2010).

Notes

1. *Father Facts*, fifth edition, National Fatherhood Initiative, 2007. http://www.fatherhood.org/organizations/programs/father-facts/overview.
2. Ibid.
3. Ibid.

Your All-in Marriage Toolset

Here are three time-tested ideas to create—or to strengthen—your marriage. You probably just want to choose one to start with that really appeals to you and will be the most meaningful to her. Pick them carefully, and be sure to take into account what will work best for your wife. Once you have selected an idea or two, implement it consistently during the next 30 days. I strongly believe that if you do, you will see a significant improvement in your marriage. And that will give you some momentum to come back to this list and choose another Put It to Work idea or two.

Relationships are a bit like a roller coaster in this way: You're either going up or you're going down (or you're about to!). Sharpen your All-in Marriage Tool by implementing some of these ideas in your own marriage. That should help you hang on safely, no matter in which direction the relationship roller coaster is moving!

As always, you will find other Put It to Work tasks for this section, and you can give us your feedback on how things worked out, at www.facebook.com/BeaBetterDadToday. I hope you will.

Idea #1: Seek a Clear Heart

If possible, get away on your own to a quiet, peaceful spot for at least two hours or so (you might want to take even more time, which is fine). Leave the time open-ended in case you need a bit more time than you thought. Bring a devotional book with you (I suggest the Bible, of course, but I'll leave that choice up to you). Be sure to bring a journal with you as well—something you can write in. And turn off any electronic gizmos. They will only be a distraction.

Use the first period of time (at least 15 minutes) to get comfortable (but not too comfortable—don't want anyone going to sleep), get rid of any distractions and get focused on the task at hand. What is that task? Looking honestly into your own heart to discover what is really there.

For sure, you (and I) are going to need help to do this. Just as neither of us can actually look at our hearts (without dying), neither can we look into our own souls accurately and objectively. But God can, and He does. So please be sure to ask Him—honestly and humbly—to help you see clearly and truthfully what is in your heart.

Use the next block of time (at least 30 minutes) to ask yourself if your wife has any competitors for your affection and love. Be honest with yourself, because that is where true growth starts. It might be another woman, it might be Internet porn, it might be a long-lost girlfriend who exists in memory only. Or it might not even be another woman—it might be your love of cars or sports. . . or whatever. Be courageous. Take an honest inventory, and write it down.

Use the next block of time (at least 30 minutes) to decide what you are going to do about each of these competitors. In short, you have two options:

1. You can leave competitors alone to flourish—crowding out your love and affection for your wife little by little. This is the easy path, certainly the path of the least resistance. But do know that if you choose this path, your marriage is probably destined for terminal decline. Just as weeds will eventually take over a garden if left untended, rivals for your attention will eventually take over your heart if you leave them unchecked.

2. You can ask God to help you clear any competitors out of your heart—and one by one think up the best way to do just that. If you've gotten too close with another woman, decide how you're going to back off

(maybe decide to write her a note telling her that because of your love for your family, you won't be able
to spend time with her anymore). If you're addicted
to Internet porn, decide that you're going to set your
Internet browser's control to disable any overtly sexual sites (it's easily done via Control Panel/Internet
Options/Content/Control/None). If you are a miser
with your wife (and/or your kids), money is probably your idol. Money, while a good servant, is a terrible master, so decide how you are going to change
that. Or maybe it's something else.

Whatever the competitor is, come up with your battle plan
and write it down. You're going to need to share your battle plan
with a close (guy) friend who will hold you accountable to actually doing it. Like any battle plan, this one is no good unless you
actually get into the fight. The person you share it with might be
your priest, pastor, chaplain or rabbi—or just a faithful, long-time
friend who can help. Write down the name of that friend and
commit to getting in touch with him.

Use the last period of time (maybe 20 minutes) to contact
your friend, tell him what you have just decided to do, and ask for
his help. If he's not there, leave him a message. Ask him to respond
as soon as he can, and be sure to get together with him ASAP.

Once you've done that, you've got your plan and you've got
an ally. Now you just need to implement the plan. This won't be
easy, but at least you've got the first two parts behind you. Just
start doing what you wrote down—and meet with your friend
every week (even via phone, email or Skype) just to be sure you're
making progress on your plan and staying faithful to it over the
long haul.

There will be plenty of temptations to go back—that I know
firsthand. But stay the course, follow through with your battle
plan and then ask God to help you keep your heart devoted to
your wife. It's the very best gift you could ever give her . . . and
your children.

Idea #2: Discover Your Wife's Likes and Dislikes and Love Her Through Them

Like all human beings, your wife has her own unique set of likes and dislikes. Some things she really, really loves (my wife loves freshly brewed coffee at the side of the bed when she wakes up in the morning), and some things she really dislikes (maybe changing a flat tire or your being late for dinner without calling). But how well do you really know your wife? I would bet that some of her actual likes and dislikes might surprise you, no matter how long you've been married.

The first part of this task is to determine how well you know your wife's likes and dislikes. First, make a list of the things you know she likes (hikes on the beach, a night out, a nice note from you, whatever). List at least 10—and hopefully you can get as many as 15 or 20. List them in rough order of her preference from most liked to least. Then do the same with her most serious dislikes (fixing a backed-up toilet, going to a football game in the rain, picking up the kids' dirty socks, whatever it is). Likewise, try to list them from the very worst to the least worst.

Now that you've got those two lists, it's time to put them to work. Take the first list, your wife's likes, and during the next 30 days don't let a day go by without doing for her at least one of those things she likes best. If you are far away from her, do the things you can now and make plans to do the rest when you are together. Make a 30-day "Blessing My Wife" calendar if you want to do so. You can schedule the harder things for a bit further out—and fill in the easier ones for the days when you are apart. Don't worry if you miss a day or two—just do the best you can. The point is to bless your wife in ways that she deeply appreciates to show her how much you love her and appreciate her.

Likewise, take a look at the other list, the things she likes to do least in life. Are there ways you could totally eliminate some of these for her? For example, if your wife is nervous about flat tires and car problems in general (and what wife isn't?), maybe you can buy her a AAA membership or something similar. Or if she hates picking up the kids' dirty laundry, make a pact with the children and pay them $10 each (or whatever) if Mom doesn't have to pick up any dirty clothes this week.

I'm sure you see what I mean on both lists. Be creative, have fun, and make it happen. Your wife will appreciate it, and you will be taking a *big* step toward being an All-In Husband.

Idea #3: Understand and Use Your Wife's Love Language

The old saying is true: every marriage is cross-cultural. I don't care if you married your childhood sweetheart who grew up in the same town as you, every husband and wife come to a marriage with a different way of expressing love and affection (and, therefore, different ways of receiving love and affection). Do you understand how to talk the talk and walk the walk that will help your wife hear your love for her? It's a sad fact that many husbands do not, and an even sadder fact that some husbands actually give up trying (effectively giving up on their marriages in the process, whether they ever get divorced or not). But, like all relationships, a good marriage is based on effective communication, and effective communication is based on being able to "speak the language" your wife understands.

If you've ever learned a foreign language, you know this: You need a teacher to help you. That's reality for all of us, from babies learning their first language to those who are learning their tenth; learning another language requires a teacher who knows that language well (for a baby the main teachers are Mom and Dad). And no one knows your wife's love language as well as she does. So ask her to teach you.

Does that idea strike fear into your bones? Do you have the courage to ask your wife to help you in this way? It's not easy; it will require you to open your heart a bit and be vulnerable (which is not always easy for us guys). But, brother, let me share a secret with you: Your wife wants you to be vulnerable to her. Not all the time, of course—and certainly not in most public situations. But women are relational, and the large majority of wives want to relate to their husbands deeply and fully. That means being vulnerable at times. Asking your wife to teach you her own secret language of love is a good step in the right direction (especially as you learn the lessons and improve your vocabulary). Check it out for yourself and see.

Loving Our Emotional Wives

Women are generally, but not always, more emotional than men. Some women are much more emotional than the average guy. Almost all women have times (usually once a month or so) when their internal biological chemistry makes them more emotional than usual. Here's a quick note on that fact, guys: We need to be thankful for it. Without your wife's monthly surge of hormones, you would not have children of your own. That's a monthly cross she bears for you and your family—and it's something we as men will never even experience. So let's be gracious, forgiving and even thankful to our wives when it's that time of month. Here are some ideas on how we can love our wives no matter what emotional state she is in:

1. When your wife breaks into tears without warning and/or cause, be sure to give her a hug and let her know how much you love her.

2. When she is worrying about being a motherly failure, as even the very best moms do at times, remind her of all the great things she has done for you and your kids. Give her a hug and tell her how much you love her (and be sure the kids do the same).

3. When your wife complains that you haven't taken care of something she asked you to do in the house last week (a

leaky faucet, a messy garage, a lawn that needs mow-
ing), get it done. It may not seem like a big deal to
you—and maybe it's not. But if it's important to your
wife, just get it done. Get your kids to help if possible,
because children need to learn to take care of their
mom too.

4. When your wife is feeling inadequate as a spouse or a
   mom or at work or whatever, be sure to listen closely to
   her. Try to figure out what is really driving those feelings. Maybe there's something you and the kids could
   be doing more of to help her. No matter what, give her
   a hug and remind her how much you love her. And let
   her know the truth: She is a good mom and a good
   wife, and you are completely committed to her.

5. When your wife gets concerned about something like
   your baby's health or your child's performance in
   school, take it seriously. Don't just say, "I'm sure it will
   be okay." If her concerns continue, get the baby to the
   doctor or go see your child's teacher. A woman's intuition is legendary for good reason. Listen to it.

6. When your wife tells you something about your current
   circumstances or your future, like, "I don't think you
   should partner with that guy" or "I don't think you should
   remain with this company for too much longer," pay
   careful attention. Don't assume your wife is mad at you
   or your potential partner or company. Your wife knows
   you better than anyone, and she wants you to succeed.
   Again, respect her intuition. If I had done that more in
   the early years of our marriage, I would have saved myself some real professional heartburn.

True Moral Compass and True Humility

Setting a high moral standard for yourself and your family—and transferring those standards to your children over time—is the most important inheritance you as a father can give to your children.

The just man walketh in his integrity: his children are blessed after him.
PROVERBS 20:7, *KJV*

My father was the one who taught us right from wrong. And that is the most important thing he could have ever done for us.
JOHN M., LOS GATOS, CALIFORNIA

If you would like to discuss any of this material via email, feel free to contact me at **gws@beabetterdadtoday.com**

In much of North America today—and throughout much of the world—it's not popular to talk about setting high moral standards. In fact, many people avoid the subject of moral standards altogether. According to American pop culture, the idea of a "moral compass" is too old-fashioned or too difficult or too constraining. However, these are the same people who moan and complain when a contractor shortchanges them or a close friend fails them or a politician gets caught lying or the CEO of a large company is convicted of cheating his shareholders. They say, "Who are these people—and why don't they know right from wrong?"

Well, these are men and women who probably grew up in homes with dads who did not have a strong moral compass for themselves or their families. And guess what? It really does matter . . . a lot.

A True Moral Compass matters for your own character and personal development, and for that of your family. Make no mistake: There is no more important gift a father can give his children than a strong moral compass. Not money or fame or houses. Not even close. No material thing will ever help guide your child when he or she has grown up and faces truly difficult moral and ethical challenges. We all know that our children will one day have to face these challenges head-on—that is certain. The decisions they make will shape their families, their careers and their very lives and those of their children (your grandchildren). Having a True Moral Compass to guide them will give them the best chance possible of leading themselves and their families on the right path.

Older people sometimes talk about what their kids are going to inherit from them. Usually they talk about money or boats or cars or homes. There's nothing wrong with wanting to bless one's children and grandchildren financially, but many of these folks are missing the point. Significant material inheritances frequently do more harm than good. Strong spiritual, moral and ethical inheritances almost always lay the foundation for a productive and successful life. That is because by far the most important things we hand down to our children—and thus to our children's children—are a strong set of values and morals to guide their lives and help them make wise decisions.

Rich or poor, all of us as parents will pass on some kind of Moral Compass to our children. The only question is this: Will it be one that works well in all settings, or will it be a "situational" compass that points in different directions depending on the situation or our personal feelings or whatever (which is the very definition of a dysfunctional compass).

Sadly, many dads today don't focus much on passing a True Moral Compass on to their children. In much of America today, too many dads have completely given up this prime responsibility. They say it's too hard. Or they're too busy. Or it's not cool. Or that others just don't understand their kids. Later in life, these same dads are "shocked, shocked" (to use a great quote from my all-time favorite movie, Casablanca) when their kids grow up to be adults who lie like a rug or cheat in business or commit adultery or whatever.

Likewise, in our society at large, many people don't like to talk about moral standards. But they are absolutely vital to the functioning of any family and culture. Think about it. What kind of family would you have if each of you repeatedly lied to one another? What kind of family would you have if your kids stole from you? What kind of family would you have if your kids could not depend on the commitment of Mom or Dad? The answers are obvious.

But think about it a little more. What kind of society would we have if everyone was constantly lying or cheating, so that no one could rely on anyone else? The answer is also very clear. In fact, there are a growing number of failed nations in our world with cultures that are all too close to that. These countries are among the poorest of the poor, in large part because no one trusts each other. The rule of law has broken down—and the law of the jungle has replaced it.

Fortunately, there are many families today who recognize the fact that the most important legacy they can pass on to their children is a strong set of ethics, solid values and timeless principles to live by. In fact, a friend of mine on the West Coast recently alerted me to a trend he is seeing out there: "ethical wills." These

The Importance of a True Moral Compass

James (not his real name) grew up in a home where he was given pretty much everything money could buy: expensive gifts, round-the-world trips, nice cars, and so on. He was even sent to an Ivy League school where his family had contributed lots of money over the years. James was given almost everything except the things that really mattered. James's dad never took the time to help him develop his own True Moral Compass. So when he got out of college and his family couldn't control him anymore, he went completely off the rails. Decades of drug and alcohol abuse later, James is a shadow of his former self. He's got a big trust fund (though he always seems to be short of money), but he is miserable. All that money, the gifts, and the material things that were given to him really didn't help at all. In fact they hurt him in the long run. But what really hurt was James's lack of a True Moral Compass to guide his decisions. Without one, he lost his way and ended up on life's rocks.

are legal documents that clearly lay out the family values that the older generation believes have been foundational in their lives. These ethical wills encourage the next generation to continue to hold and practice these values so that they will be able to pass on an inheritance of moral and ethical strength to their children as well. Overall, that sounds like a good idea. Anything we can do as dads to help our children develop a True Moral Compass is a very good thing.

Unfortunately, there are way too many dads today who think that someone else is supposed to teach their children right and wrong. Teachers, pastors, coaches, guidance counselors and others can be important allies in this effort, but they are not equipped—nor are they able—to do it by themselves. Certainly our children need to have good role models outside the family (we will talk about the importance of "Other Good Dads" in Tool #8). But throughout time, in cultures all over the world, it has always been one of the primary jobs of the father (and mother) to teach their children the difference between right and wrong. That job has not changed today, and it is our responsibility as fathers to lead in this important work.

Now, I'm not saying that if Mom and Dad do their very best their kids will not make mistakes. Everyone makes mistakes. In fact, just like us, our kids can make huge mistakes. That's why Tool #4, "Heartfelt Love," is so important. As God's Word teaches, "Love covers over a multitude of sins [including mistakes]" (1 Peter 4:8, *NIV*). But one thing is clear across cultures and across continents: If we as dads do our best to set high moral standards for our families—both in word and deed—our kids will have a much better chance of developing a strong moral backbone themselves. In fact, the Bible gives an interesting promise to all dads (and moms) who may be wondering about this:

> Train up a child in the way he should go, even when he is old he will not depart from it (Proverbs 22:6, *NASB*).

That's a profound verse—and one that is frequently misunderstood. Note that it does not say, "Your children will never make a mistake" or "Your kids will be perfect teenagers." No, it says that if we train up our children (and certainly that has to include helping them to truly understand right and wrong), when they are adults they will remember those lessons and not depart from them.

The "rule of law" starts at home, and it starts with us as dads. We must live up to the rules we set down (in agreement with Mom) in our households. If we break one of those rules, we should admit it and ask our family to forgive us. That is the only way the rule of law works: It is either true for everyone or it is true for no one. Once we establish the basic rules by which our home is governed, we must ensure that they are understood and followed—"understood" because no one is going to follow a rule they don't understand, and "followed" because a rule is not a rule unless it is true for everyone.

Once our children understand the basic rules, they will test them. That is where we must apply appropriate discipline. I know that parental discipline is not a popular subject today, but trust me, all love with no discipline can be as much of a disaster as all discipline with no love. Both of the extremes are fatal to a family. But the happy medium, 10 parts love to 1 part discipline, is a good rule of thumb. Consistent, age-appropriate discipline is absolutely necessary. In fact, I will go so far as to say that your children's success in the future depends on it.

Dare to Discipline

Consistent, age-appropriate discipline is so important to our children's future that it probably deserves its own chapter, if not its own book. It is certainly a tool that we should be using, always with wisdom and care, to help our children develop their own True Moral Compass. As adults, we know (or certainly should know) that our actions have real consequences. That's one of the most important things we can teach our children, because when they come into this world, they are oblivious to that fact. Over time it is up to us to ensure that our children understand that their actions—both positive and negative—will have very real consequences. Making wise decisions based on that understanding is one of the definitions of what it is to be a mature adult.

In fact, research demonstrates that one of the many important benefits of setting boundaries and limits for our children is that they gain a sense of security and contentment. As many childhood psychologists will tell you, children whose parents do not give them reasonable limits and boundaries seldom report being "content" in their later lives.

But how do we consistently set the right limits for our children and apply age-appropriate discipline in a wise and effective way? That is the subject of entire books—and there are some very good ones on that subject, such as *The New Dare to Discipline* by Dr. James C. Dobson and *Rock-Solid Kids* by Larry Fowler. I would recommend reading either of these books, but for now let's touch on just 12 basic rules for effective discipline.

1. The Goal of All Discipline Is to Teach Your Children, Not Punish Them

Always remember that the primary goal of discipline is to teach your children, not to punish them. This cannot be said too often. Sometimes, especially when our kids fail to understand that what they did was wrong, discipline must involve an appropriate punishment (a time-out, grounding, a loss of driving privileges, whatever best fits the situation). But the goal of all discipline should be to teach your children right and wrong, and that almost always requires a good explanation of what he or she did wrong, why it was wrong and what he or she needs to do to make it right (clean up the mess, go to Mom and ask her forgiveness, pay for whatever got broken, and so on). Punishment without a clear explanation of what the child did wrong, and why it is wrong, is both "cruel and unusual."

2. Never Discipline in Anger

Sure, you might be angry that your child just broke your best watch or your cell phone or your golf club. That's understandable. But remember, it's your son (or daughter), and you can always get another watch or cell phone or golf club. So while it's okay to get angry, it's not okay to discipline your child out of anger. And let me be clear about something here: Never, ever hit your kids (or anyone else in your family). Never. I know for most dads that is not an issue, but you'd be surprised how much child abuse (and spousal abuse) still goes on today. So I just want to be 100 percent clear about that: no hitting, ever. Don't discipline in anger; it won't achieve the result you seek.

3. Use the Appropriate Consequences for the Level of Wrongdoing

Be sure that the discipline you impose is appropriate to the act and age and maturity level of your son or daughter. If you apply huge punishments for relatively minor wrongdoing, what are you going to do if your child does something seriously wrong? Or if you consistently fail to discipline—or apply only light discipline when serious discipline is needed—how is your son or daughter going to learn that his or her actions have real consequences?

4. Be Consistent, Fair and Evenhanded in Your Discipline

My kids are always saying, "You are much easier on so and so than you are on me." But my wife and I have truly done everything we could to be consistent and fair with all of our children. Heaven help us if that had not been the case. All of us know friends who feel, in some cases perhaps rightly so, that their parents favored an older brother or younger sister . . . or whomever. They feel that they were less loved and are, therefore, less lovable. Some people never get over that. So let's not burden our kids with even the slightest element of favoritism. We need to love each and every one of our kids fully and equally—and we need to discipline each of them in the same way.

5. Up the Ante When Disciplinary Consequences Do Not Work

Employ an escalating standard of discipline to repeated wrongdoings, especially if they grow in seriousness. Again, children need to understand that their actions have consequences. So if one of our children is repeating the same behavior over and over—despite our best attempts to lovingly discipline and teach him (or her) the error of his ways—it may be time to up the ante. I'm not talking about going ballistic the second time your child breaks a house rule, but I am saying that if your son or daughter is exhibiting the same problematic behavior over and over, it is probably time to go to the next level of discipline. He or she needs to understand that the behavior is not acceptable and needs to be changed. It may also be time to get professional help. There are many fine family counselors in the U.S. today who can—and do—regularly help families who need it. There's absolutely nothing wrong with seeking professional help with your children, if needed. In fact, it can be super-helpful.

6. Let Your Yes Be Yes and Your No Be No . . . Together

Stay united with your children's mother on your approach to discipline. One of the worst situations when it comes to discipline is when Mom and Dad openly differ about how to discipline their child. Or if Mom (or Dad) quickly gives in to the kids' demands time after time. Our kids are smart. Don't think they won't notice substantial differences of opinion—or the tendency to easily cave in—and use it to their own benefit.

It's hard to deal with statements such as, "Dad, why are you so tough on me about that? Mom doesn't mind at all when I . . ." Of course, you may have a legitimate difference of opinion about how or whether to discipline your kids for a particular wrongdoing. But work it out with her privately, and if that's not possible for any reason, agree that you will back each other (at least in front of the kids). Presenting a united front on the discipline issues will make it much easier for you and, ultimately, for your kids as well.

Parents who regularly let their no become yes are just encouraging their kids' negative behavior. So do everything you can to be united with your children's mother on the discipline front and make sure your yes means yes and your no means no . . . together. It's not always easy, but it does pay big dividends over time.

7. Take the Lead on the Discipline Front

Brother, let's face the facts: Moms are usually (much) better than we are on the nurturing front. Thank God for that. But usually it is up to us to lay down the rules in the family and make sure they are followed. When the rules get broken, which will happen as our children test those rules, it is (most frequently) going to be up to us as dads to ensure that our kids understand what they did wrong, why it was wrong and what they need to do to make it right. Fortunately, we are well equipped for this important job; we just have to go about it consistently, wisely and with the full support of our children's mother. This is not a job we can outsource to anyone else or wish away. It is one of our most important roles as fathers, and we must execute it.

8. Give More Praise than Correction

Be sure to ladle out 10 times as much positive reinforcement as you do discipline. When you catch your kids doing something right, let them know how much you appreciate it. That positive reinforcement will help your children know that you are watching not just to catch them when they do something wrong but also to praise them when they do something good. It will also make it much more likely that you will see that positive behavior more often, and, most important, it will help build your child's self-esteem on something that is real.

Too many parenting books today talk about "building Johnny's self-esteem" based on false praise and empty words. When our son gets a C on a math test because he didn't study, he doesn't need to hear how smart he is and what a great student he is, or what a lousy teacher he has, or other excuses. He needs to hear that he must study harder the next time. But when he gets an A (or, for some students, a B+) on a test because he studied hard and prepared well, he needs to hear how truly proud we are of him. Ten parts love and praise for every one part discipline is a pretty good balance. If you don't see your kids daily, ask your wife (or children's mother), family members and caregivers to keep you informed about your children's accomplishments, no matter how small. When you have the opportunity, praise them for these accomplishments.

9. Tailor the Discipline to Fit the Child

Tailor your discipline to each child, because each child is different. If you have both boys and girls, you already know what I'm talking about. But even between your sons—or your daughters—there exist important emotional (and age) differences. So while you must always try to be evenhanded and fair with discipline, you must also tailor the discipline to fit the child. For example, one of our sons is a bit of an introvert. He likes to be by himself, and he needs his alone time. Another of our sons is the exact opposite; he loves being with people and hates to be out of the conversation. For these two, who have many other things in common, the most effective discipline for each is quite different. And it needs to be.

10. Cooperate with Other Authority Figures in Your Child's Life

Be sure to work in tandem with the other authority figures in your children's life. Close communication and cooperation with your spouse and with teachers, coaches, pastors, youth workers and other good adults who have an authority role in your kid's life can be helpful for three main reasons. First, it can clue you in to an attitude or behavior you hadn't really noticed but needs to be dealt with. Second, if you agree as a team to focus together on a particular behavior or issue, you are that much more likely to succeed. Third, it is good to share the discipline role. You, as dad, don't want to always be the heavy, and when your son or daughter hears the same thing from teachers as they do from you and Mom, it makes an impact.

11. Do Not Assign a Discipline Role to Older Children or Extended Family Members

Don't put it on your older children to discipline their younger siblings. It is simply too much responsibility for the older children, no matter how mature they might be. It also opens up a Pandora's Box of potential problems, including possible injury or deeply hurt feelings. Of course, the older brother or sister should encourage younger siblings to act appropriately—that is critical. But when it comes to discipline, that should be the responsibility of Mom and Dad . . . period. The same goes for uncles, aunts, nieces, nephews, grandparents, and so on. They can—and should—help by being good role models and encouraging proper behavior, but only you and your children's mother should be the disciplinarians.

12. Stick Up for Your Kids

Your children need to see you as their defender and protector, not just as someone dishing out discipline. I'm not saying you should argue with the umpire in Little League when he mistakenly calls your son out at home. Our kids need to learn about the real world—and shielding them from it is actually harmful. But if one of your younger kids is (for example) being repeatedly bullied or mistreated at school (or anywhere), it is your job to set that right and make sure it does not happen again. Not only will your kids be deeply appreciative, but it will also help them realize that the basic rules of civilized behavior are for everyone—and that they are good.

A Tragic Story of a Former Neighbor

Years ago, we lived down the street from a couple who would literally let their children do anything. Some of our more "free thinking" neighbors applauded these parents. "How trusting" or "How forward leaning," they would say.

The daughter became friends with our daughter—and so we got a glimpse of the reality behind the veil. In truth, the reason the kids were left to do whatever they wanted was that the parents were rarely home and didn't seem to care at all about their kids. As a result, the kids were neither well loved nor well disciplined. The little girl would frequently (believe it or not) come to our door in the rain, asking if she could get out of the cold. Her stories left us shaking our heads. Sometimes neither parent would be at the house when she got home from school—or for hours thereafter—and they would forget to give her a key. Other times, she would come over and ask for dinner; her parents had gone out and had not left any food in the kitchen. We took care of her as best we could, and she clearly appreciated it.

We eventually moved from that neighborhood, but a few years later I saw that same girl when I went back to visit some other neighbors. It was clear that she was highly medicated, and our friends told me that she was in and out of institutions. She had been a bright, charming little girl just looking for love and warmth and someone who cared enough about her to show her right from wrong. Unfortunately, her father, who died of a drug-induced heart attack a few years later, didn't care enough about his little girl to be that man, and neither did her mom. Sadly, our daughter's little friend paid for their selfishness and self-centeredness with her own life.

Fair and effective discipline is important, because we must teach our children one of the basic realities of life: Actions (both good and bad) generate consequences. Some parents try to shield their children from this reality. In its extreme form, these parents are called "enablers." Don't be an enabler of unacceptable behavior from your children. Show them the right path, with plenty of love and praise mixed in with a little bit of discipline when needed. Ten parts love/praise to every part discipline is a good mix.

We must never forget that discipline is not an end in itself and should never be done in anger. Discipline is an important tool to help our children develop a True Moral Compass. As dads, we must set the example by developing and using our own Moral Compass effectively. Our kids watch everything we do—and they remember. That's why "do as I say, and not as I do" is a recipe for parental failure. Those dads who talk the talk *and* walk the talk are the ones who will effectively pass on a strong set of values and ethics to their children. That is one of the most important gifts a man can give to his children.

The Value of Humility

We all make mistakes; no one's Moral Compass is right 100 percent of the time. That's where humility comes in. Humility is a manly virtue, even if we don't hear about it much these days. But what is true humility? And why is it important for us as fathers? Of course, there are many good definitions of humility, but one I like a lot is this: *an accurate understanding of reality, of my place in God's universe, and my true strengths and weaknesses.*

Why is this important? Because an accurate understanding of our place in God's universe tells us that while we are individually important and deeply loved, we are no more important and no more (or less) loved than our neighbor. So, when things are going well, a good sense of humility will keep us from believing our own press releases. And when things are going badly, a good sense of humility will remind us that we all make mistakes and that, despite those mistakes, we are still important and valued.

True Humility Is an Asset

My friend Scott has taught me a lot about humility. Even though he is a smart guy, he is also one of the most honestly humble men I know. That has been a great asset for him in his professional life, where he has been extremely successful. But even more important, it has helped him to be a great husband and a wonderful father. He's faced more than his share of challenges, trials and failures, but he's been able to be honest with his wife and kids about his mistakes. He's allowed his family to truly know who he is and who he isn't. Scott's commitment to humility and transparency has helped him and his family to turn a few of life's more serious lemons into lemonade, and it has helped his children to understand that an occasional failure doesn't mean you throw your Moral Compass out the window. You might have to recalibrate it, and you might have to do some serious soul-searching to set it right again, but it still remains one of the most important assets that human beings have. In fact, a True Moral Compass and a real sense of humility are two of the things that make us fully human in the first place.

A true sense of humility is important for all of us dads, because it allows us to admit when we are wrong. That is extremely valuable for each of us, because we all make mistakes on the fatherhood front. In fact, by definition, being a dad means making mistakes. But that is equally true of our children—and they know it. So when our children see us make a mistake, and we quickly take responsibility for it and work to put it right, they learn how to deal with their own errors and failures and even those of others.

It's vital that we pass on to each of our children a True Moral Compass and a true sense of humility—two of the greatest legacies we can leave them. They are much more important than money or houses or anything material. For with them, your children can chart their own course in this ever-changing world and access the humility to make mid-course corrections when needed.

For Further Reflection

1. Do you agree that a True Moral Compass is one of the most important legacies you, as a dad, give your children? Why or why not? What would you need to do to improve the accuracy of your own Moral Compass?

2. How close would you say you and your children's mother are to the 10/1 Rule (10 parts love per one part discipline)? What do you need to do to get closer?

3. Are you and your children's mother usually united on the discipline front? Is your "yes" yes and your "no" no? In other words, do you set a firm line of right and wrong and stick to it? Or do you (or she) usually give in after the kids whine or complain enough?

Today's Quick Wins

1. Take 60 seconds to think forward to your burial service and what you'd like people to say about you. Honor, integrity, dependability and kindness . . . isn't that how you want to be known?

2. Take 60 seconds to think about what people would honestly say about you if you died today.

3. Starting today, work on becoming the kind of man you want to be known as for the rest of your life. Don't forget to ask God to help you. Trust me, the God of the Bible loves to answer prayers like this.

Your True Moral Compass and True Humility Toolset

How do you as a father set a high moral standard for yourself and your family and make it stick? At its core, this is a leadership question, and good leadership always requires that you start with yourself. "Do as I say, not as I do" is a recipe for disaster as a leader, and that is very much true for us as dads. So let's start by examining your own Moral Compass and make sure it is working properly.

Check Your Moral Compass

Please answer the following questions sincerely, honestly and to the best of your ability:

1. Do you have a high moral standard? Do you live it in front of your family?

2. Are those standards derived from a timeless external source (such as the Ten Commandments) that has proven itself trustworthy over thousands of years? Or are they really more about what's best for you in any given situation?

3. Do you and your children's mother share the same moral standards?

4. Do you and your children's mother clearly and consistently communicate those standards by word and deed to your children?

5. Is your own behavior consistent with those standards?

6. When you make a mistake (as we all do), are you quick to acknowledge it, seek forgiveness, clean up any mess you have made and ask for God's strength and courage not to repeat it?

7. Are you developing friendships with other men who share these values and who will help you stay the course when things get tough?

If you can truly answer yes to these seven key questions, congratulations! You are on a good road. Developing a True Moral Compass within yourself is the first step to helping your children develop their own. But don't get overconfident. Developing your own True Moral Compass is a job that is never completed. You can always refine and strengthen it, and you must.

Remember that key rule of life: We are either going forward or are going backward. There is no standing still. That's one of the biggest dangers of pride, or overconfidence: It can get us thinking that we are okay where we are, that we don't have to push higher up and farther on. That would be a big mistake. In fact, pride (or overconfidence) is frequently what happens right before we take a big fall—often of the moral type.

Think of the former governor of New York (a Democrat born to privilege) who was at the height of his power when he, though married to a beautiful and intelligent southern belle who had borne him four beautiful daughters, had an extended affair with a high school dropout who was a drug addict and a prostitute. It destroyed his career. Or consider the former governor of South Carolina (a Republican who had been deeply blessed by his wife's wealth, connections and intelligence) who got sucked into an affair with a middle-aged Argentine woman who wasn't half as attractive as his wife. Career and family destroyed . . . permanently.

My point here is not to ring up a couple of politicians. There are plenty of CEOs and other regular guys just like you and me who have gone down that path to disaster right after saying, "I'm at the top of my game." In fact, as men it's when we're at the "top of our game" that we have to be the most cautious about overconfidence. As the Bible wisely teaches, "Pride goeth before destruction" (Proverbs 16:18, *KJV*).

The truth is this: If not for God's grace, our family's love, the help of our friends and a True Moral Compass, we could all be in the very same boat as the politicians mentioned above. We need to be honest about that. If we, as fathers and as men, know how susceptible we are to moral failings, it will help us to avoid doing the little things that can so often lead to gigantic failures down the line. It will also help us to push on in life, to further refine and improve our own Moral Compass so that we can pass the very best on to our children.

Help for Walking the Walk

If you answered no to one or more of the seven questions, thank you for being honest. It's impossible to fix something until you admit it isn't working right. Now that you've done the hardest part of the work (admitting there is a problem), we can work together to put it right.

Please get together with a trusted friend. Be honest with him about your answers to the questions above. Ask for his help—and prayers—to become the type of father you know in your heart that you want to be. Sin loves darkness and hypocrisy, but when we expose it to light and truth, its power is diminished. If we continue to treat our sin with honesty, courage and faith—with the help of friends and family—by God's grace it will heal. If you have questions, let me know at www.facebook.com/BeaBetter Dad Today.

Talk the Walk

If your True Moral Compass is working well—and you're spending quality time with your kids—they will internalize a lot of what they see in you. That's just how kids learn. But it's not enough just to walk the talk. You're also going to have to talk the walk to help your kids understand that their actions have consequences and where they might have gone off the rails. This generally involves discipline, which is a tool we are going to have to be willing and able to use if we hope to see our children develop their own True Moral Compass.

The 10/1 Rule

We've talked in this chapter about the importance of discipline and what I call the 10/1 Rule (10 parts love for every one part discipline). The following are five examples of ways to show your children love, appreciation and praise when you notice them doing something good:

1. Send your child a text message or email—or maybe even write a letter and mail it. Let your child know how much you appreciated something specific that he or she did or accomplished lately.

2. Crown that particular son or daughter the "Winner of the Day" and explain to the whole family why he or she won the prize. Maybe there is a small gift involved, maybe not. That's up to you. What's important is the public recognition of the good action.

3. Let your child know that you noticed the good behavior or achievement, and as a result, he or she has earned some special reward or treat.

4. Grab your son or daughter the next time you see them and give them a really big hug, or do something that he or she loves to do. Let the child know how proud you are of his or her good action.

5. Write a special letter, create a certificate of achievement or make something for your child—and let him or her know that you noticed the good behavior.

Here are five examples of ways to discipline your children appropriately when they have made a mistake (always remember to explain clearly up front what he or she did that was wrong *and* why it was wrong):

1. Provide a direct verbal explanation of how much he or she has disappointed you—and what will happen if that first-time behavior is repeated. Note that this can work with

sensitive children, but not always. It frequently does not work for high-spirited children. If it does not work, you must impose the threatened discipline for the second offense. Let your yes be yes and your no be no—or you're in trouble on the discipline front.

2. Add chores or responsibilities appropriate to the child's age and what he or she did wrong (for example, washing the dishes every night for a week, or walking the dogs by himself, or cleaning up junior's room, or whatever).

3. Assess a financial penalty appropriate to the child's allowance (if he gets one) and the level of the problem. This is usually effective when the children are old enough to understand the value of money (approximately 10 years old and older).

4. Take away privileges appropriate to the child's age and level of discipline (a time-out for an hour, or no sleepovers for a month, or no use of the car for 30 days, or no use of the computer for 72 hours, and so on).

5. For severe, repeat issues, enact more extreme disciplinary measures. For example, a teenager who repeatedly steals little things might need a visit from the police to help him or her recognize the seriousness of the problem. Again, seek professional help if your child is exhibiting serious behavioral and/or moral issues like constant lying, cheating and/or stealing. These may well be symptoms of larger issues that you will need professional help dealing with.

Be united with your wife or children's mother on the discipline front, and be sure that you are both walking the talk and talking the walk. When you help your children develop a True Moral Compass and True Humility, you will give them a powerful blessing both now and throughout their lives.

TOOL #4

Heartfelt Love

It is through commitment, fidelity, grace and tenderness that you show your family—in word and in deed—how much you love them (and therefore how valuable they are to you . . . and to God).

Love covers a multitude of sins.
1 PETER 4:8, *ESV*

I grew up in a home without a lot of love. So learning to truly love my wife and our children took time. But little by little over the years, God has helped me to understand what real love is—and to use it in my family. And that has made a big, big difference.
DAN W., McLEAN, VIRGINIA

If you would like to discuss any of this material via email, feel free to contact me at **gws@beabetterdadtoday.com**

Loving your family every day is one of those easy-to-say-but-hard-to-do-each-day things. But it sure is important. In fact, heartfelt love in a family is like oil in a car's engine. It won't last long without it.

Love is a much-used word, but it has many meanings and is frequently misused. Most of the time we hear the word "love" used in a romantic sense, and certainly that is part of what I mean here. But there are other aspects of the word that are even more relevant to the family. These comprise four elements of the Heartfelt Love Tool that we need to focus on and develop: commitment, fidelity, grace and tenderness.

Commitment

Family love is nothing if it is not committed. You might have grown up in a situation where your father was not really committed to his family. I did. Sometimes you could count on him, but other times you could not. Sometimes he was there, but other times he was not. This kind of behavior from a father hurts, and it stunts a child's ability to trust. The best families are always built on commitment. As the leaders of our homes, we must cultivate and demonstrate that commitment in thought, word and deed.

One of the first things to realize about commitment is that it takes time. As we discussed earlier, most children spell love "T-I-M-E." Those old excuses that overly busy dads like to pull out of their bag of justifications—such as claiming "it's quality time that counts"—doesn't give the full picture. Of course quality time counts, but the only way you get consistent quality time is if you're willing to make quantity time. Sure, you might get lucky once in a while. But just like any gold miner will tell you, you've got to spend a lot of time panning to find the gold.

Commitment is as much a decision of the will and an attitude of the mind as it is a feeling of the heart. In fact, when feelings of love take a holiday (and they will), your will and attitude are what keep you in the fight. They are the backbone of long-term commitment. And commitment is one of the cornerstones of every successful family.

I think most of us instinctively know this. Even the terms of the traditional marriage vows speak to the importance of commitment: "For richer or for poorer, in sickness and in health, as long as we both shall live." If we think about it for a moment, we can see why this is so important; and not just to our families, but also to ourselves and the society in which we live.

For Wives, Children and Even Grandchildren

A husband's commitment to his wife and children is the foundation of a stable family structure. With commitment, they can be secure in the fact that the person closest to them in the whole world is not going to leave them or abandon them, no matter what happens. This makes for far more confident, strong and capable children emotionally, academically and socially . . . indeed, along every dimension. These strengths continue into adulthood and make the child of a healthy marriage much more likely to have a good marriage later on than those peers who were victims of divorce in their childhood.

The data strongly backs this up: Marriages in which either spouse comes from a divorced family are twice as likely to fail as marriages in which neither spouse came from a divorced family. Marriages in which both spouses come from divorced families are more than three times more likely to fail.[1] The effects of divorce carry across the generations. Even grandchildren whose grandparents divorced had lower levels of education, higher levels of marital discord and lower quality relationships with their parents, on average, than their peers whose grandparents did not divorce.[2] Once again, if you are divorced, don't give up hope. While there is no getting around the fact that divorce causes damage in families, you can work to minimize that damage by putting the tools in this book to work, working in partnership with your children's mother, and being the best dad you can be.

For Ourselves

A wife's long-term commitment to her husband is usually (but not always) a reflection of his long-term commitment to her. Remember, guys: It is almost always men who end up in the wheelchair or the walker first. Do you want to be on your own then? No, you do not. Here's the secret we looked at earlier: In honoring our commitment to our families, we become stronger and deeper men—better men, in fact, than we would have been had we taken the easy way out and dumped our commitments when times got tough (as they invariably do at points along the way).

If you need further proof of this, here is some data. According to a nationwide study conducted in the U.S. in 2005, 65 percent of ex-husbands and 78 percent of ex-wives listed lack of commitment as their main reason for divorce; 62 percent of both divorced men and women wished they had worked harder at their marriage. Almost two-thirds of men said they felt that getting a divorce had been a mistake.[3]

For Our Society, Neighborhoods, Workplaces and Faith Communities

The benefits of committed families are clear on these points: Children from committed two-parent homes are more emotionally and psychologically secure, have more stable friendships, get better grades, are more likely to go to college, are more likely to lead productive professional careers, and are much more likely to have healthy, committed families themselves. On the other hand, children from broken homes are much more likely to drop out of school, suffer mental illness, be convicted of a felony, spend time in jail, and repeat the whole cycle again by being absentee fathers or single moms with multiple children by different fathers.[4]

As Senator Daniel Patrick Moynihan wrote prophetically back in the 1960s: "From the wild Irish slums of the nineteenth-century Eastern Seaboard to the riot-torn suburbs of L.A., there is one unmistakable lesson in American history: A community that allows a large number of young men to grow up in broken families dominated by [single mothers], never acquiring any stable relationship to male authority, never acquiring any rational expectations about the future—that community asks for and gets chaos."[5] Brother, we need to do our part to ensure this is not the future of our family, our society or our nation.

We will take a closer look at how to develop greater commitment to our family in the Put It to Work Guide at the end of this chapter.

Fidelity

It is no coincidence that one of the clearest and most often-repeated warnings in both the Old and New Testaments is the warning against marital infidelity. The James Bond image of "a girl in every port" might look cool on the big screen, but in real life it guarantees long-term alienation from one's family (and, I would argue, eventual loneliness and emptiness for oneself).

You know the U.S. Marine's lifetime motto: *Semper Fidelis* (or *Semper Fi*). It means "always faithful." Every U.S. Marine (and I would say every U.S. serviceman and woman) understands that the success of the team and the success of the mission depend on his willingness to put the team and the mission above his own self-interest. *Semper Fi* is also the motto of every truly great dad.

If you are married, fidelity to your wife is more than just staying out of an adulterous sexual relationship (although that is an absolute essential); it means being faithful to her in other ways as well. Do you tend to put your wife down with your friends when she's not around? Many guys do—and that is a dangerous habit. Have you ever grown emotionally attached to another woman, even though there was no sex involved? That's a bit like a Marine jumping out of his foxhole and running around screaming, "Shoot me! Shoot me." Eventually, that guy is going to get hit. How about how you treat your wife, both in public and in private? *Semper Fi* means never, ever making a joke at her expense or making her feel like a second-class citizen. You would not want her to do it to you, would you? It's up to you to set the tone for your family; that's what a leader does.

There are a number of elements to fidelity, and each one supports the other. For example, if you treat your wife with respect and dignity in public and private, you are less likely to have an extramarital affair. Why? Because in doing so you will meet her need to be cherished, and she will more readily meet your needs (hence less pressure or interest in sex outside marriage). Put it to work for yourself and see what happens. But remember, human beings don't change overnight. These things take time. No matter what happens, do not commit emotional or physical adultery against your wife, for that will likely be the end of your marriage.

You might be thinking, *Wow, this fidelity stuff is hard.* Yes, in our sex-crazed culture, it is not easy. We need help—all of us. That's why Marines don't fight alone; they fight in teams. We will study in detail the importance of close friends and mentors when we look at Tool #8, "Other Good Dads," but for now it bears repeating: *Semper Fi* (Always Faithful) is the watchword of all good dads. Think about the power of those two simple words.

At this point you might be thinking, *I've already blown it.* If that's the case, you've got a serious problem. I don't think I am overstating the case when I say that unfaithfulness in a marriage is like cancer in a body. Either you do something radical to get rid of the cancer, or it will kill you. Likewise, either you get rid of infidelity, or it will kill your marriage. It is no accident that the Bible makes clear that the only legitimate reason for divorce is infidelity—and let me be clear: I believe that infidelity includes physical and/or emotional abuse.

Jesus Himself taught us that God hates divorce. But Jesus also said that the only legitimate reason for divorce is infidelity. There's a reason for that. So if you have fallen to the temptations of the flesh outside your marriage, please recognize that you need to deal with this serious problem right now. There are no easy answers to infidelity—the best solution is not to go there in the first place— but if you've got that problem, get help and deal with it before it kills your marriage.

If you have remained faithful to your wife and family, I have three words for you: "congratulations" and "thank you."

I say "congratulations" because you are on your way to showing yourself a faithful man and establishing a legacy of faithfulness in your family for generations to come. Think about that. Do you want your children, grandchildren or great-grandchildren cheating on their wives and families? Of course not. Establishing a legacy of faithfulness is probably the most important thing you can do today to prevent unfaithfulness in future generations.

I say "thank you" because our world needs more men like you. We have plenty of rich guys, plenty of famous athletes, and more than enough "celebrities." But faithful men of character and integrity—men who set a high bar for their children and keep to it themselves—is one of our world's most pressing needs today. So thank you, thank you, thank you. Keep up the great work! I hope you will help me and other men by sharing with us some of your secrets to a faithful marriage at www.facebook.com/BeaBetterDad Today. We would love to hear from you, encourage you and to be encouraged by you.

Grace

"Grace" isn't a word we hear much of today in our culture. It's a word that was much used by our forefathers but sounds a bit old-fashioned to many of us. Nevertheless, it is an important word and one that we need to practice as dads. Grace is "undeserved mercy" or "undeserved compassion" or even "undeserved love." It is the love that God shows to us in spite of our shortcomings when we have a personal relationship with Him through Jesus Christ. Notice the word "undeserved" in the definition. That's the key element of grace, and it's why it is an important quality in every family relationship.

It's key because all of us—*all* of us—mess up. Our kids break our favorite fly fishing rod or our iPod. Or our wife has her third fender bender . . . in three months. Or we lose our temper (and we as dads have to be careful about that, because words spoken in the heat of the moment can have serious long-term consequences). What I'm trying to say here is simply this: We all mess up. The Bible calls it sin or selfishness, and I happen to agree that we are all born with a sinful (i.e., selfish) nature. If you have children, you've certainly noticed that they did not come into the world with a how-can-I-help-others attitude. Quite the opposite, in fact.

Because we all mess up from time to time, we all need grace (undeserved mercy or forgiveness) from those around us. That starts with our family. Of course, if we want to benefit from the grace of our family when we mess up, we must show our family members grace when they disappoint us. In fact, as the head of our homes, it is up to us to set the example. It won't take long in marriage for us to have the opportunity to show grace to our wives, and that is doubly true when we start having children. Each time we show grace—true grace—to a family member, we strengthen the very foundation on which our family is built.

Why is that? It is because grace is one of the best tools we have to show how much we love the other person. Let's face it: If some stranger came into your home and broke your iPod or golf club or car, you'd call the police and have him arrested (and rightly so). But family members are not strangers—not at all. So when they do the same thing, it is a great opportunity for you to put grace to work. I'm not saying you need to smile and ask them to break your other golf clubs. I am saying that you need to use that situation as a "loving moment" toward your wife or children's mother or a "teaching moment" for your child.

A Loving Moment and a Teaching Moment

A "loving moment" is one in which you say something along these lines: "It's true that I'm a bit upset that you had an accident [or whatever]. But you are way more important than that car, and we can have it repaired. So don't worry about it; I'm just glad you're safe and sound." If you can pull out grace in that situation instead of getting angry or sarcastic (which happened a great deal in my house when I was growing up), you will be making a big deposit in what I call the "Marriage Bank." Those deposits usually come with interest, so the next time you mess up she will be much more likely to show you the beauty of the grace from the receiving end.

A "teaching moment" is one where you sit down with your son or daughter when he or she has done something significantly wrong to help your child clearly understand and acknowledge three things:

1. What he or she did that was wrong and why it was wrong.

2. Why he or she needs to ask for forgiveness, do his or her best to put it right and, if needed, suffer the appropriate consequences (take a look at the section called "Dare to Discipline" in Tool #3, "True Moral Compass and True Humility").

3. That you still love him or her very much, and you just want to help your child be the very best boy or girl that he or she can possibly be.

That is a perfect use of grace, and if you can use it in that situation instead of humiliation or anger, you will build up assets in what I call the "Family Bank." And it's important to make as many deposits as you can to the Family Bank while your kids are young, because you will be making many "withdrawals"—such as enforcing curfews and dress rules and dating rules—when your kids hit their teen years.

Grace is one of the most powerful yet underused tools we have as fathers. That's probably because many of us weren't shown a lot of grace when we were young. Also, men in cultures around the world generally do not pride themselves on being "men of grace." But that doesn't make it any less important as a fatherhood tool. In fact, its relative scarcity in our modern world might make it even more important.

God's Grace in Our Lives

If you sense that you are lacking in grace, that might be because you don't realize how much grace your heavenly Father has for you. Let's face it: If we feel unloved (and grace is really just love in action), it will be hard for us to love others (even our own family). This is why it is so important for each of us to understand—and truly know—God's grace in our own lives. So take a minute right now to think about the fact that God Himself came to earth to take the full penalty for all of our sins onto His own back. That is grace indeed. You might have heard that a million times in church—or this might be the first time you've ever heard it—but take a couple of minutes to really meditate on that reality. If you are loved to

Showing Grace in Adapting to Family Changes

A dear friend of mine sent this story about the importance of showing grace to our family members when they are going through an important change in their lives, such as going away to college. He writes, "It was the day before the Jewish New Year began—Rosh Hashanah, the most important family day of the year—and for the first time in 19 years, we were not together as a family. My oldest son, Aaron, was in his freshman year. There were so many emotions for his mother and me to deal with, and as we got closer to the holiday, there was no phone call from Aaron. We wondered what this meant. Was Aaron okay? Did he still love us? Should we call him? Or would that be setting a wrong precedent? There were so many unknowns for us.

"Thank God, we decided to call Aaron, and we had a great conversation with him. As it turns out, he was just super busy with his new friends and new classes and integrating into his new environment. Later, after the Holiday, I had the opportunity to go to New York and have dinner with Aaron. So many great things came out of our conversation. Of course he still loved us and was thinking of us. His mother and I just needed to be a bit more sensitive to his new situation in life and think not only about how things had been in the past (living under the same roof) but also his new reality. In other words, we needed to understand that things for our family had changed and extend grace to Aaron as he got used to his new environment.

"I pointed out to Aaron that these communications with his mother and me were still so important to us, so we came up with a plan. Every Friday afternoon, when Jews say a special prayer to bless their children before the Sabbath (Jacob's Prayer), we agreed that no matter where he was in the world, we would speak together and I would bless him. He would also spend some time on the phone with his mother. Of course, we speak all the time, but now this 'scheduled' time means a week does not go by without our being involved in each other's lives."

that extent (and you are), you need to understand that and take joy from it.

Note that just like beautiful Christmas gifts around the tree, the gift of God's grace has to be opened if you are to really know what it is. So, if you don't know personally in your heart of hearts how much your heavenly Father loves you, take the next few minutes to ask Him to forgive your sins (His grace for you). That is why Jesus came to earth: to demonstrate once and for all God's extravagant and extraordinary love for you. But you have to unwrap that gift by opening your heart to God's love and grace. It doesn't matter if you've been a Christian for years or if this is the first time you've ever asked God to show His love and grace to you by forgiving your sins—just meditate on His eternal and everlasting love for you personally. That is grace, brother, and He will fill up your soul with it if you allow Him to do so.

Not only will God's love and grace bring you deep and true joy (because it is so important to be loved), but it will also allow you to show love and grace to others much more easily. Like a beautiful fountain that is overflowing with clean, pure water on a hot day, God wants your life to be overflowing with love and grace for others, especially for your family. That will simply be impossible if your own soul is not being filled up regularly by His love and grace.

So be sure that you are truly in touch with God's grace in your life. God doesn't love you because of what you can do or will do or have done for Him (you absolutely, positively cannot bribe God). He loves you just because He loves you. His gift of grace is available to us today through the death of Christ on the cross, and He offers it to everyone equally with absolutely no regard to race, language, looks, income, religion or anything. Yes, He will pay the whole tab—everything you owe—but you have to admit your sinful nature and ask Him to forgive you and change you. That takes courage. So, if you've never done it before, please ask God to come into your heart, be the Lord of your life, forgive your sins and make you a better and stronger man. He will. He wants His love and grace to flow into you and through you, like an eternal fountain of life-giving love for your own soul and those around you.

If you've been a Christian for some time, but your "grace fountain" has gotten clogged up, this is the day to get it working properly. No matter what has stopped up your fountain (maybe it's the cares and worries of this world that have stolen away your joy), please kneel right now and ask the Lord to clean out the blockage. Repent of any known sin, and ask Him to help you live in victory. That is His goal for all His people: to have your grace fountain flowing free and clear once again. Once you have God's life-giving love flowing again into your heart and life, you will have so much more grace for your family and indeed for everyone you meet. Jesus' statement in Luke 6:45, "For out of the abundance of the heart [a person's] mouth speaks" (*ESV*), is as true today as it was 2,000 years ago.

So try to use this tool of grace the next time your family members disappoint you. They might be amazed; they will certainly be thankful and appreciative. Let's face it: The physical damage is already done. The car is in the shop or the camera is broken, and they probably feel really bad about it already. Getting angry is not going to fix the problem. In fact, it almost always makes the situation worse.

Tenderness

I admit that "tenderness" is probably not in the Marine dictionary, but you must develop this essential fatherhood tool if you are to truly love your family. Everyone who has been alive for more than 10 years knows instinctively that there are huge differences between men and women (and between adults and children). These differences manifest themselves in many ways: in how we deal with stress, in the way we approach relationships, in how we handle crisis. But, in almost every case, women are programmed (both biologically and spiritually, I believe) to act in ways that are more tender and nurturing than men. And, as you know if you've been a husband for any length of time, almost all women react to a tender, nurturing approach better than the approach of a Marine drill sergeant.

Hopefully, you've never treated your wife or children's mother in the way a drill sergeant treats his cadets. But what I'm saying here is that there is a wide range of approaches to almost any situation in life, and generally, we men will take the more direct, action-oriented route. It's the "get it done" approach. That approach is not necessarily wrong; if we didn't take that approach at our jobs and in our relations with other men, we'd probably be in for a rough time. But that is exactly why we have to consciously work on developing tenderness as part of our Heartfelt Love Tool.

Very few of us have been encouraged to develop tenderness in our lives. In fact, for some of us, tenderness might need the most sharpening of all. It is not easy to face our families after a long day of dealing with the world and pick up the tenderness tool. But that is a crucial part of truly loving your family. They are not your crummy boss or your overbearing co-worker, and they are certainly not your employees. They are not even your buddies. Not at all. They are your family, your own flesh and blood. By the way, for all those dads who have adopted or inherited children, I very much believe that in the deepest sense of these words, children you have adopted or inherited become (over time and through your love and care for them) your own flesh and blood.

Net-net: If you try to use the same approach with your family as you do at work or when you're with your friends, you are not going to be successful. Period. You can make a lot of excuses about the stress and pressure of work or the people you have to deal with, but the truth is the truth. You must develop a gentler, humbler, more nurturing approach with your family if you are to be truly an effective husband and dad. There is no other way.

Here's the good news: Each of us, even the toughest of us, has a gentle side as well. I know that is true because once, even if it was a long time ago, we were each tender little boys, with hopes and dreams and fears, who wanted to be cuddled, loved and praised. Even if that part of you has been dormant for a long time, it is still there, and your family needs to see it. You will be amazed at how positively they react to it. And, brother, here is a deep truth for you: You need to nurture that part of you, because that is one of the elements of every man's soul that helps make him fully human and fully alive.

Some guys think they can never be "weak," and I admit that in the business world, doing so can be a career-limiting move. But we are not talking about the business world; we are talking about our families. They need to see all of you, not just the strong and tough parts but the sensitive and uncertain parts as well. Trust me, if done in the right way at the right time, your family will love you all the more for baring your soul to them in this way. They will be able to know you more deeply and love you more fully. That is what marriage and family is all about—really knowing another human being deep down, and loving that human being, weaknesses and all.

Learn Your Child's Love Language

Bruce, from the Midwest, states, "An important part of being a hands-on dad has been learning how different my children are in terms of their particular 'love language.' Each of our three boys has different needs, ranging from appropriate physical touch, verbal affirmation and undivided attention to playing sports and games together and reading good books together. Each child is a distinct individual with specific gifts, talents, temperament and personality. I've learned to maximize whatever time I have with my kids. I realize I still have much to learn, and it is an ongoing journey to be the best father I can be. But I have no doubt the journey is worth all the time, talent and treasure in the irreplaceable role God has given each of us to be the best fathers we can be."

Most of us need help putting all four elements of the Heartfelt Love Tool into regular practice. That's why I've placed a Put It to Work Guide at the end of this chapter that has been specifically designed to help you sharpen and use this tool more frequently.

Please be sure to check it out for yourself. I will be right there with you, because I've got a lot to learn on this front myself.

For Further Reflection

1. How important would you say the Heartfelt Love Tool is for the average family? How important is it for your family?

2. Which of the four elements of the Heartfelt Love Tool do you feel are your strongest? Why? Which elements do you feel are your weakest? Why?

3. Do you have the courage to ask your family about that? What did you learn from their feedback?

Today's Quick Wins

1. Take 60 seconds to think about a time when you felt deeply and totally loved (maybe from childhood or on a special day in your life). What did you feel?

2. If you are married, take 60 seconds to remember when your wife first told you she loved you. How did that make you feel?

3. Take 5 minutes right now and, either through an email or letter, tell your family members sincerely and from the heart how much you love them. It is in your power to help them feel deeply and truly loved today and every day, from this day forward. Use that power now . . . while you can.

Notes

1. Nicholas H. Wolfinger, "Family Structure Homogamy: The Effects of Parental Divorce on Partner Selection and Marital Stability," *Social Science Research*, no. 32, March 2003, pp. 80-97.

2. Paul Amato and Jacob Cheadle, "The Long Reach of Divorce: Divorce and Child Well-being Across Three Generations," *Journal of Marriage and Family,* February 2005, pp. 191-215.

3. "A National Survey on Marriage in America," from National Fatherhood Initiative, Gaithersburg, MD, 2005.

4. *Father Facts,* fifth edition, National Fatherhood Initiative, 2007. http://www.father hood.org/ organizations/programs/father-facts/overview.

5. "The Case for National Action," U.S. Department of Labor, 1965.

Put It to Work Guide

Your Heartfelt Love Toolset

We've looked at the four elements of the Heartfelt Love Tool: commitment, fidelity, grace and tenderness. Let's now examine how we can strengthen and sharpen each of these important elements to use in your relationships with each member of your family.

Commitment is a decision of the will that only you can make. No one can make it for you. How committed are you to your marriage and your family? Let me give you three choices: (1) very committed, (2) moderately committed, and (3) not very committed. Please choose one.

If you chose "very committed," good for you. Commitment is the foundation of any marriage and every strong family. Without commitment, the long-term trust, deep confidence and personal security that are the hallmarks of all good families simply cannot grow. But even if you did choose "very committed," do a simple test to validate that answer. Look at how you spent your time during the past few months. What does it tell you? No matter what you might say you are committed to, the way in which you spend your time will reveal what you are actually committed to.

Even if you are not with your family on a day-to-day basis, do you spend some time thinking about them, praying for them, communicating with them, or perhaps making small gifts for them? Are you remembering their birthdays and soccer games and piano recitals? If you're not doing these things, I've got bad news for you: You're not very committed to your family. That's just reality. But there's good news, too: You can make the change. Begin to prioritize time with your family. Keep your promises. Skype them, if possible, to be there to read a bedtime story to the kids. Be present in whatever way you can, and don't miss out on an opportunity to spend time with them and do things together.

If you're not doing these things, I've got bad news for you: You're not very committed to your family. That's just reality. But there's good news, too: You can make the change. Begin to prioritize time with your family. Make it home for dinner, or at least be there in time to read a bedtime story to the kids and tuck them in. Maybe get them up and make breakfast together in the mornings (or at least on Saturdays). And be there on weekends and special days; holidays and birthdays are hugely important.

As we've talked about already, kids spell love T-I-M-E. If you really want to be a very committed dad—and that is super important—you're going to have to make T-I-M-E for your family. There is no other way.

Three Ways to Sharpen Your Family Commitment

Here are three ways that you can begin to use and sharpen your family commitment tool today:

1. *Keep your word.* This sounds easy, but in our change-a-minute world, it's easy to let your family commitments be the ones that get changed first. Even if you do not live with your children, if you make plans to be at your daughter's high school play, be there. If you've promised your son a trip to the zoo, do it. In 50 years, you won't even remember what kept you so busy, but your son and/or daughter will remember whether or not you came to his or her games, plays or concerts.

2. *Change your priorities in favor of your family.* Don't miss out on an opportunity to do a puzzle or play a board game with your kids . . . or help them with homework. If you love to read the Sunday paper, get your kids to each read an article, and then present it and discuss it with them. You get the idea.

3. *Commit to quantity and quality time with your family.* Spending quantity time with our family might be difficult for some us, but we still need to commit to doing it whenever possible. Instead of doing something with your buddies, suggest that everyone bring their kids. You and your buddies will probably have an even better time—and your kids certainly will.

Fidelity has much in common with the All-in Marriage Tool we looked at in detail in Tool #2. Being a *Semper Fi* dad is a huge asset when you're trying to build a happy family. But *Semper Fi* dads, just like *Semper Fi* Marines, are made and not born. So what will it take for you to be a *Semper Fi* dad?

Three Ways to Strengthen Your Dependability

Dependability is a big part of fidelity. Can you remember times in the past when you did not act in a dependable way toward your family? Can your family trust you to do what you say and say what you will do? If this is a problem for you, thank you for being honest about it (many men are in denial on this issue—and it is slowly killing their marriages and/or their relationships with their kids). If your dependability tool is bent (or broken), you've got to get it fixed. Here are three steps that can help you repair it:

1. *Confess your shortcomings and ask forgiveness of your family.* I know this is not easy, but trust me; it is an essential first step. Don't think for a moment that your son wasn't crushed when you didn't show up for his game as you'd promised, or that your daughter wasn't hurt when you forgot to pick her up after school. If you've got a problem with dependability, your family already knows it. Asking them to forgive you and to help you get it right going forward is a big step in the right direction.

2. *Let your yes be yes and your no be no.* In other words, do not commit to anything you aren't sure you can do. Some dads seem to think that saying they will be somewhere—and then not going—is better than saying up front, "Sweetheart, I am going to be busy that day and I just won't be able to make it." In fact, it is much better to be up front and honest about what you can and cannot do—this is not just true with your family, but with everyone. The old saying about "under-promise and over-deliver" is 100 percent true. So practice under-promising and over-delivering on your commitments to your family. It will greatly strengthen your dependability.

3. *Get a memory aid if you need one.* Mark a calendar or place sticky notes where you can see them often to remind you of your promises. If you have a cell phone, use the alarm system to remind you of your promise to your family. For me, the calendar on my smart phone is a great memory tool. I set an alarm for an hour (or two) before any important event. When it rings, it reminds me of the upcoming event and helps me not to be late (or forget about it entirely). It works for me, but maybe you have a better idea. That's fine. The basic idea is clear: If you've committed to do something, write it down and do whatever you need to do to keep the commitment.

Using one or all of these three steps will help you strengthen your dependability, and that's a big part of the Fidelity toolset.

Three Ways to Strengthen Your Grace

As I mentioned in this chapter, grace is not a big part of the Marine's lexicon, but it is a very important toolset for all dads. There are three main ways that you can strengthen grace in your life:

1. *Remember the times when grace has been extended to you and how grateful you were.* If you were lucky, you had parents and/or grandparents who were people of grace. If not, perhaps you had someone in your life as a young person (a teacher, a Cub Scout leader, a coach) who was clearly a person of grace. Hopefully, someone extended grace to you when you were young. Even if there was very little grace in your childhood, you need to think about the grace that God has shown you by coming down to earth to pay for your sins on the cross.

2. *Remember that you are not perfect—or even close to it.* Why is that important? Because if you look at yourself honestly, you can see how much grace you need. If you are honest with yourself, you will see that you will need your family's grace in the future many times over. If you use grace now, you will be much more likely to receive their grace when you need it in the future. This is undoubtedly why Jesus taught us in Matthew 6:12 to ask God to give us grace in the same measure that we have grace for others ("Forgive us our sins as we forgive those who sin against us" [*NLT*]). Net-net: If you truly understand how much grace you need from others, you are much more likely to show grace yourself.

3. *Look for opportunities to show grace.* I am not by nature a person whom anyone would describe as being "full of grace." I'm more of a driver, a "get it done now" kind of guy. A lot of guys are. That's why I've got to be on the lookout for opportunities to use grace. Maybe that would be when my son or daughter did something that cost our family a fair amount of money. Or if someone interrupted me at a meeting to ask a silly question. Or a bad driver cut me off on the highway. Or maybe when a telemarketer calls in the middle of dinner to sell me something. The point is that there are many

opportunities every day to use and strengthen the grace tool, and I need to look for those opportunities—and use them to strengthen my grace tool (because, naturally, it is pretty darn weak). Like any tool, the more I use it, the more comfortable I am with it. Maybe you're like me. So let's start today. Let's ask God to help us grow in grace, and let's look for opportunities to put grace to work. Over time you will see grace grow stronger and more powerful in you, and that will be a huge benefit for you, not just with your family but with friends, colleagues and neighbors as well.

Three Ways to Empower Tenderness

Tenderness (also called kindness) is another element of the Heartfelt Love Tool that many of us guys aren't overly familiar with. And that's understandable. But if we want our families to be tender and kind to us and to each other, we must learn to use it effectively.

As the leader of your family, you set the tone at home. When Mom is down in the dumps, the way you respond to her is going to set an important example for your children. Do not fool yourself—they are always watching. Likewise, when one of your kids messes up but is truly sorry and asks humbly to be forgiven, it is important to roll out the tenderness tool to embrace him or her and clearly show how much you love him or her.

For most of us, tenderness is inappropriate at the office or in the barracks or at the shop. So we don't use it there much, if at all. That's why it's important to occasionally take a few minutes to destress. Leave behind whatever happened during your day. And remember that your family members are not your colleagues, your boss or your subordinates, and that they deserve your tenderness.

Tenderness is primarily used in verbal conversation. So let me ask you: Are your words seasoned with tenderness when you speak to your family? It needs to be. Tenderness is a balm that makes relationships better. Even if your wife or children's mother isn't always tenderhearted with you, you are the one who needs to change and be kind. Even though past experience may have taught you that it is useless to be tender, give it another try. If you continue being tender, over a period of time your family will begin to respond positively as they begin to trust that what they are seeing is the new and real you. Trust me, if you lead in this, your family will follow. It might take some time, especially if you've not exhibited much tenderness in the past years.

As the old saying goes, "kindness is on the tongue of the wise," so be wise and ask God to help you guard your tongue at home, starting today. Here are three ways that you might be able to do this more effectively:

1. *Count to 10 before responding to any harsh word from a family member.* Remember: A gentle answer can help avoid a huge argument.

2. *Take time to notice if anyone in your family is having a rough day.* Ask them about it, be sure to listen carefully, and give a hug if needed. Just by asking you will be using tenderness, and you may well help turn her or his day around.

3. *Stop and smell the roses.* Take time to tell your family members that you love them. Thank God for them and for this day, enjoy the beauty of it, thank Him for His tenderness to you.

Many of these elements in the Heartfelt Love Tool—commitment, fidelity, grace and tenderness—are closely related. As you begin to practice with one element of the toolset, you will find it easier to use the others. As you begin to use the Heartfelt Love Tool actively and effectively over time, you will notice a big change at home. As the Bible teaches us, "Love covers a multitude of sins" (1 Peter 4:8, *ESV*). So don't worry if you've made a mistake; we all have. Just continue to develop your Heartfelt Love Tool so you can rely on it to cover those mistakes, because, as God's Word also teaches us, in the end "love never fails" (1 Corinthians 13:8, *NIV*).

TOOL #5

Empowering Servant Leadership

Empowering your family by putting their needs above your own will yield rich benefits today . . . and for generations to come. This is the essence of great fatherhood.

The Son of Man did not come to be served, but to serve, and to give His life a ransom for many.
MATTHEW 20:28, *NASB*

Don't ever doubt the impact that fathers have on children. Children with strongly committed fathers learn about trust early on. They learn about trust with their hearts. They learn they're wanted, that they have value, that they can afford to be secure and confident and set their sights high. They get the encouragement they need to keep going through the rough spots in life. Boys learn from their fathers how to be fathers. I learned all those things from my own father, and I count my blessings.

FORMER VICE PRESIDENT AL GORE, SPEAKING AT THE
THIRD ANNUAL NATIONAL SUMMIT ON FATHERHOOD
IN WASHINGTON, DC, JUNE 2, 2000

If you would like to discuss any of this material via email,
feel free to contact me at **gws@beabetterdadtoday.com**

The Empowering Servant Leadership Tool is another absolutely critical tool for us as dads. It is the essence of all great leadership, but one that is not easy to develop in our "me first" culture. Courage and will are a big part of this tool, because putting your family's needs and wants above your own is, when you come right down to it, a matter of the will . . . and courage.

There's nothing easy about saying no to what you want in order to put your family's needs first. In fact, from our earliets days our culture feeds us with a steady diet of "me first and the heck with everyone else." So, becoming an empowering servant leader means swimming upstream from the flow of where most of society is moving.

Maybe you had a mother and/or a father who readily sacrificed for you. If you did, I trust you realize how much you owe them. Sacrificial love is a powerful thing—in every culture and for all time. This is the type of love that Jesus, a poor itinerant Jewish carpenter who died on a cross 2,000 years ago outside the walls of Jerusalem, exhibited for us. Today, almost half the world celebrates, in some form or fashion, the death of this man who sacrificed His life for the sins of the world. Just think about that for a minute. Whether you are a believer or not, it's mind-boggling. It shows us both the power of God and the power of sacrificial love, which is at the heart of servant leadership.

Jesus as a Servant Leader

Jesus is the perfect example of an empowering servant leader. He put His own interests second—and His Father's will and our interests first. A lot of religious leaders over the centuries have talked about God's love, but Jesus actually showed that love firsthand. Today, He gives us the power to show that same type of love to our families, which is why if you don't know the power of Christ's love personally in your own life, you are missing out on the most significant power for good in this world. For how else can we love others unless we ourselves know that our heavenly Father loves us?

As I said, even if you're not a believer, there is much to learn from Jesus' powerful lessons in empowering student leadership. After all, He took a rag-tag bunch of poor, uneducated working men and made these complete nobodies into the leaders of a movement that went on to change the known world. In doing this, He modeled some of the key principles of the Empowering Servant Leadership Tool for us. Many of these principles are similar to the Ten Tools we have been discussing in this book.

Leading by Example

A good friend of mine who lives in the Washington, DC, area—where most homeowners hire small caravans of service workers to maintain their lawns—recently sent the following story to me: "Growing up in Houston, one of my earliest memories as a young boy was waking up Saturday morning to the sound of a lawn mower outside my window. Peering outside, I would see my father, pushing the mower, cutting our grass. He would remain outside for a few hours doing yard work while my brother, sister and I watched Saturday morning cartoons. When he was done, he would come inside and make hot dogs for our lunch.

"As I watched my father, I learned that many of the comforts our family enjoyed (such as a well-tended lawn where we played) came as a direct result of his labor and servant-like attitude. For that reason, I mow my own lawn every Saturday morning and take special pride when I see my two young sons watching me from the window. Instead of them growing up thinking that receiving services from others is how things get done, I want my sons to appreciate the value of hard work, sweat, using their hands, bodily strength and taking care of their own responsibilities—not just paying someone else to do it for you.

"To my surprise and delight, my wonderful wife gave our eldest son a play mower for his second birthday. It quickly became his favorite toy. He loves to take it outside and mow the lawn, just like his daddy."

In fact, it is pretty clear that Jesus was a master of all 10 of the Tools of Fatherhood. He obviously put His Family First (that is, you and me and all of His people). His death on the cross was the perfect example of putting our interests before His own. He also was All-in for His Mission here on earth—His Noble Vision, if you would. He clearly had a True Moral Compass and True Humility, and He made it a priority to pass those on to His disciples. His Heartfelt Love was legendary . . . and still is today. He practiced Empowering Servant Leadership all the time.

Jesus also exhibited the tools that we will discuss in upcoming chapters. He was clearly a man who built Relationships that Worked. We see in Jesus' prayers and in the way He lived His life that He asked for Heaven's Help all the time. He had Other Good Men around Him, and He made it a priority to build into their lives. He definitely had an Optimistic, Never-Surrender Attitude, even in the face of death, defeat and disaster. He remained steadfast and quietly confident that good would triumph in the end. Finally, He was clearly devoted to Dynamic, Whole-Person Support. He understood the strengths and weaknesses of each of His disciples and provided each one with a different mix of emotional, spiritual, mental and physical support.

I think it is safe to say that if you come to master the Ten Tools of Fatherhood, you will become a strong, empowering servant leader for your family. If you feel you need help in this area, I urge you to ask God for His help via His Holy Spirit. I know that for some this might seem like a strange suggestion. But as we will talk about in Tool #7, "Heaven's Help," it makes sense to ask your heavenly Father to help you be a better earthly father. He can—and will—help you grow as an Empowering Servant Leader for your family if you ask Him sincerely and diligently to help you. He promises to answer this type of prayer (see James 5:16). He also promises to develop an ever-deeper sense of His love and peace and joy in your own heart . . . no matter what the circumstances (see Galatians 5:22).

All of us need the power of love in our hearts. This is especially true for those of us who did not grow up in a household where sacrificial love was frequently on display. Unfortunately, sacrificial love for one's family seems to have gone out of style in many parts of America in the last generation or two. Today, we as individuals, as families and as a nation, are paying the price for that.

Sacrificial love is a key component of the Empowering Servant Leadership Tool. It is just as important today as it ever was—and maybe even more important, given the disintegration of so many other social pillars of our society. But one thing is for sure: It is a critical skill in the Ten Tools of Fatherhood.

As a dad, you will likely have regular opportunities to put your family's wants and needs above your own, and thus show in a very

A Great Picture of Empowering Servant Leadership

Do you remember the 1992 Summer Olympics in Barcelona? Derek Redmond was one of the UK's best sprinters. With the help and support of his dad, Jim, and his entire family, Derek had trained all his life for the chance to win an Olympic gold medal, and he was one of the favorites in the 400-meter. He was running the race of his life at the Olympics until he pulled a hamstring midway through and crumpled to the track. While most people (even world-class athletes) would have stayed down, Derek decided to get back up and try to finish the race. He could hardly use his left leg, and the pain on his face was clear to see.

After about 30 yards, when it looked like he was about to give up, Derek's dad broke through the security cordon and ran to his son's side. He put his arm around Derek and allowed his son to use him as a left leg. They completed the race together in what has become one of the all-time great Olympic moments. Derek Redmond didn't win a medal, but he won the salute of millions by having the courage to get back up. And his father, Jim, gave us all a great example of using the Empowering Servant Leadership Tool when he almost literally carried his son on his back to help him complete his dream.

real way your sacrificial love for your family that is at the heart of the Empowering Servant Leadership Tool. Some of these opportunities may include the following:

1. *Daily acts of service:* This might take some creative thinking on your part depending on your particular situation. However, regardless of the distance or the circumstances, there are still opportunities every day to serve your family in small ways. The key is to understand which act means the most to your family and to focus on those.

2. *Putting your family's priorities first in both big and little things:* Perhaps in the past you have not put our family's priorities first. Today can be a new beginning, and it begins in your mind. Think about some ways in which you can put your family's needs above your own. Maybe you planned to buy a new piece of clothing for yourself, but you know your son needs a winter coat. What would a servant-leader do?

   Every day, in big ways and small, you have opportunities to practice your Empowering Servant Leadership Tool by putting your family's desires ahead of your own. As the leader of your family, you set the primary example. So if you want your children to be servant leaders for their families tomorrow, you need to be a servant leader to your family today.

3. *Pointing your family to their heavenly Father:* It will take guts for you as a dad to admit that you don't have all the answers—and it will take even more guts to point your family to the One who does. Again, Jesus is a great example here. He never bragged or boasted about His own power, wisdom and authority, but always gave all the credit to His heavenly Father, and He pointed His followers to the Holy Spirit for long-term help and guidance. In doing so, He set the stage for

His small, powerless band of followers to literally change the world, a result no one foresaw and few can adequately explain (apart from supernatural assistance) even today.

You won't always have all the answers, and you won't be with your children every minute for the rest of their lives (in fact, you will probably be gone from this earth long before they are). So isn't it wise to take a page out of Jesus' playbook and point your family members to their heavenly Father who does have the answers? And to also point them to the Holy Spirit, who can minister power and love and joy to them every day for the rest of their lives? That is true servant leadership that will empower them forever.

Using the Empowering Servant Leadership Tool effectively does not mean saying yes to everything your family wants all the time. As a dad, you have to be the one to say "no more candy" or "no more TV" or "no more going out with those friends" when you know that is in your children's best interest. But it does mean putting your family's long-term best interests first in front of your own in the three ways we've just discussed.

I know from personal experience that this isn't an easy thing to do consistently. But I also know that if you ask God to help you become a strong servant leader for your family, He will answer your prayer. He was the perfect servant leader here on earth, and He promised to give the power of His Holy Spirit to anyone who wants to become a better servant leader. So just ask Him yourself, sincerely and honestly, to help you become a better servant leader for your family, and see what happens.

Finally, don't forget the Put It to Work Guide at the end of this chapter and the additional tools and services found at www.Fellow shipOfFathers.com. Each Put It to Work Guide is designed to help you sharpen and use more effectively the tool you've just read about in the chapter. The Put It to Work Guide in this chapter is one of my favorites.

For Further Reflection

1. On a 1 to 10 scale, with 1 being the best, how would you rate yourself in terms of using the Empowering Servant Leader Tool in your home?

2. What grade would your family give you? Were their ratings similar to yours, or did they widely vary from yours? What can you learn from them?

3. What opportunities do you have to demonstrate Empowering Servant Leadership on a regular basis? Will you do it?

Today's Quick Wins

1. Take 60 seconds to remember the best boss/coach/teacher you ever had. Think about how he or she helped you grow both as an employee/player/student and as a person.

2. Take 60 seconds to reflect on times when your mom or dad or grandparents helped empower you when you were young. Remember how it felt.

3. Take 60 seconds to meditate on some ways your family members (if they are old enough) try to serve you. Remember how good it feels when your family really helps you (or even when they just try hard to do so).

Put It to Work Guide

Your Empowering Servant Leadership Toolset

As I mentioned in this chapter, we don't see a lot of empowering servant leadership these days. We hear a lot about it in certain circles, but we don't see a lot of it in action. That's because true servant leadership is usually difficult to do . . . and always personally costly. But that's exactly why it is so important. In any organization, from a platoon to a company to a family, leadership sets the tone. If the leader is willing to serve the greater good of the organization, it will usually prosper. If not, you'll usually end up with a lot of quarreling and unhealthy relationships.

So how do you develop and strengthen your Empowering Servant Leadership Tool? Here are three things you can do:

1. *Identify three opportunities to demonstrate empowering servant leadership in your family—and put yourself into them.* Maybe your son is struggling at school and needs your help to establish good homework habits. Maybe your daughter needs advice about buying her first car. No matter if you are close to or far from your family, there are opportunities to put your Empowering Servant Leadership Tool to work. . . if you look for them.

2. *Once you've begun to sharpen your own Empowering Servant Leadership Tool, talk to your family members about it.* Let your family know that this tool is for every member of the family . . . not just for Mom and Dad. Encourage

each of them to look for opportunities to serve each other, and be sure to praise them warmly (or reward them in other ways) when you find them doing so. Also be sure to recognize and appreciate your wife's or children's mother's service, not just when she serves you but also when she is serving the kids. Most importantly, keep using your own Empowering Servant Leadership Tool to serve them. They will notice and will emulate your efforts.

3. *Ask God—and your closest friends—to encourage you to continue to develop your Empowering Servant Leadership Tool.* You're probably going to need His help, and theirs, to continue to sharpen this tool. As you become more comfortable with performing servant leadership, you will probably see other service opportunities you had never noticed before.

The reality is that there might not be a big response from your family at first, so you might especially appreciate outside encouragement. But no matter what, keep looking for opportunities to engage your Empowering Servant Leadership Tool on behalf of your family. You will be building a stronger family and a better future every time you put this tool to work.

TOOL #6

Relationship Tools that Work

To be good a dad, you also need the willingness to listen, the skill to truly hear, and the ability to relate deeply with your family.

I felt he never heard what I was really saying. He always wanted to fix the problem. I just wanted him to listen to me.
AMY, DIVORCED MOTHER OF THREE,
TALKING ABOUT HER EX-HUSBAND

It makes all the difference in the world when I know that my husband has really heard me and understands me.
MARIA D., HAPPILY MARRIED MOTHER OF FOUR

If you would like to discuss any of this material via email,
feel free to contact me at **gws@beabetterdadtoday.com**

As men we like to take action. However, to be good dads, we also need the willingness to listen carefully, the skill to truly hear, and the ability to relate deeply with our wives and children. This set of what I call Relationship (or Relational) Tools is of critical importance to being a good dad, and it is no accident that it follows the Empowering Servant Leadership Tool we discussed in the last chapter. We will not be able to really serve our families unless we are willing to carefully listen to and truly hear what they are saying to us. Certainly we can't expect our family to be open with us and share with us their deepest hopes and dreams and fears unless we prove ourselves able to listen to them, truly hear them, and relate deeply with them.

Relational Tools in the Ten Tools of Fatherhood include these three critical skills: (1) the willingness to listen carefully to your family members; (2) the ability to actively understand the deeper message behind the words; and (3) the gift of being able to deeply relate to each family member. Let's briefly look at each of these.

The Willingness to Listen Carefully

Careful listening is mostly a matter of the will. It means putting other matters aside and making an intellectual effort to listen fully and intently to what a family member is saying to you. Men, this is not something that most of us are very good at doing. We're busy, we've got lots to worry about, and we don't have time for "whatever it is my family member wants to talk about for the umpteenth time." If we have an attitude like that, is it any surprise that our family members confide in us less and less . . . or maybe not at all?

Here's a suggestion to get things going in the right direction. Starting today, make time to engage in careful listening. If you are not with your family right now, you can practice careful listening with those around you. It might just be for a few minutes, while some days it might be longer. For those of us who haven't been truly listening to our family members for a while, it is going to take time just to get them to open up again. But if you make the effort and you truly listen to them about their struggles, their fears, their hopes and dreams—you will witness some amazing results over time.

How can you know if you are a careful listener on a consistent basis? Here are some simple questions for you to think about and answer:

- Do you often find yourself thinking about something else while others are speaking?
- Do you rush to get your own thoughts into the mix, thereby cutting them off in mid-sentence all too frequently?
- Does your mind wander and you lose track of the conversation from time to time?
- Are you frequently tempted to look over their shoulder at someone else, or look at the TV, your iPhone or Blackberry in the middle of the conversation?

If you answered yes to any of these questions, then you've got a problem. Fortunately, there is an answer to this problem, because we can all learn the art of careful listening. It is an important part of the Relational Toolset, so it is critical that we each learn how to use it effectively.

Ask Good Questions

One good careful listening skill is the art of the good question. I don't just mean asking, "How was your day?" (although that's a good place to start). I'm talking deep, important questions that show your family you've been paying attention to things that matter to them . . . and you care. These include questions like:

- "What happened with that friend you felt was mean to you the last time you saw her?"
- "How are you feeling about _____ now?"
- "Wow, I am really sorry that happened. It's tough when [fill in the details] takes place. Is there anything I can do to help?"
- "What do you think we should do?"
- "How's it going at work [or school, or whatever]? How did you do on that big project/midterm/report recently?"

Net-net: Sincere questions that build on things your family members share with you show them you are actively listening, that you understand that part of their lives, and that you care about them.

A Cautionary Tale

Zach and his wife (whom we'll call Lisa) had been married for more than 30 years, until a very bitter divorce a few years back. Zach had been a hard worker and a good provider for the family; he loved his job and was very good at it. He had travelled extensively almost every week, while his wife had stayed at home with their two children. Their little girl had a learning disability that was a major challenge, and their boy had some serious health issues as well. Both Zach and his wife were Christians and neither believed in divorce, though they (quite understandably) struggled with God over the "unfair" burdens their beloved children had been given.

When the couple's son went off to college, Zach noticed that their communication declined in both quantity and quality. More and more, she had her own life with her own friends—as did he. Zach thought it might be a good idea to do something to change the slow erosion, but he never got around to really talking with Lisa about what they should do (and, to be honest, she was difficult to pin down on tough issues, preferring to stick to "everything's fine" surface conversations).

The couple's communication continued to deteriorate to the point where they rarely talked about anything beyond the superficial and the children. Not surprisingly, their level of physical intimacy paralleled their level of relational intimacy until it, too, reached virtually zero. Zach was lonely and depressed, so he threw himself more and more into his work to compensate. Lisa spent more and more time at her work and with her girlfriends. Neither moved to change things—so things didn't change. In the end, while neither Zach nor Lisa wanted or believed in divorce, that was what ended their marriage. It devastated their children.

While I am all for the "Never Surrender" attitude that we will explore in Tool #9, let's not fool ourselves into thinking, *I'll never get a divorce,* or, *Divorce just can't happen to me.* It can and might if you fail to work on your marriage, and this often starts with communication. And if you're already divorced, you know how just difficult it is on everyone involved. So let's learn from experience—and do whatever it takes to not make the same mistakes twice. So build stronger and better relationships with our wives and children . . . every single day that we can.

Follow Up After the Conversation

Another great way to demonstrate careful listening is to write your son or daughter a short note or email about your conversation shortly afterwards. Let her or him know in writing that what was shared with you really touched your heart. Say how thankful you are to be his or her dad. Also, be sure to let them know that you will be praying for that specific challenge or area, and then be sure to follow up in a week or so to say that what she or he shared is still on your heart and mind. Trust me, your family will notice your effective use of careful listening and will appreciate it.

Of course, each family member is different. Your 9-year-old will relate to you in a very different way from your 16-year-old. But each member of your family will deeply appreciate the sincere interest you show by using careful listening. And as your relationship blossoms over time, with the practice of careful listening, you will be able to understand not just the words that are spoken but also the true meaning behind those words and the person who is speaking them. That skill, which I call "active understanding," is another important tool in the Relationship Toolset.

Slowly but surely, if you keep up the discipline of careful listening on a regular basis, you will see your family members open up their hearts to you. That is one of the greatest privileges a father can have. Sure, it will take time—it might even take a good deal of time if you've been short or lacking for years in the communication department—but, like a flower that is carefully tended and watered, over time they will open up to you. And that is a beautiful thing.

The Skill of Active Understanding

Active understanding builds directly on careful listening. It is the art of not just hearing the words being used but also understanding the message behind those words. This is a skill that is based on careful listening that develops over time. In fact, it is a skill that grows directly out of careful listening, and it is a vital skill for all effective dads. You and I both need it in our fatherhood toolsets. Why is that?

We need it because it is the only way that we can ever truly understand our family members. Every human being is unique, and each of us is different in ways small and (sometimes) large. But the English language, like all languages, has a standard set of words that mean different things depending on who is using them and in what way. The only way to truly understand the deeper messages behind the words is to understand the speaker, the context in which he or she is speaking, and what he or she has said before on that and related subjects. That requires a common history of previous conversations.

This is why careful listening is so important. Over time, it gives us the context and knowledge of our family in a way that helps us truly understand the message behind the words. That, in turn, gives us the ability to continually deepen our active understanding of our loved ones, which, in turn, leads directly to the third Relationship Tool that every effective dad needs: the ability to deeply relate to our family members and deepen and grow those relationships over time.

The Ability to Deeply Relate

This is the most important of the Relational Tools. It is the tool that binds families together over time, and out of it springs mutual respect, affection and understanding. However, it only works with the constant application of careful listening and active understanding.

Here's a truth about us human beings: We are either growing, or we are dying. That is true both for us personally and for our most important relationships. Either we are moving forward—growing in our character, in the fullness of our humanity and into the person that God Almighty created us to be—or we are going backward. In life there is no standing still, and that is also true for our most important relationships. Either we are growing closer over time, generating more understanding and more empathy toward our family, or we are growing farther away from them.

Please do not misunderstand me; the art of building deep, long-term relationships with those we love is a life-long process. Like all processes, it involves flawed human beings and has its ups and downs—and sometimes those ups and downs can be pretty severe. But over a period of months and years, the direction of our relationships can be clearly seen. If we are married, the goal for each of us as husbands over time is to be growing closer to our wife— while she grows closer to us. This is possible if we use the tools in our Relational Toolsets.

As the father in your household, it is up to you to take the initiative in these relational skills. You will most likely be able to count on your wife or children's mother to help you, because by nature most women are relationship-oriented. But just as an organization takes on the character of its leader over time, your family will take its primary cues from you as a dad. If you sharpen and use your Relationship Tools well, as time passes you will come to truly understand and love each member of your family in a deeper way. You will also be setting a great example for your kids and their families to come. Best of all, you will have the joy of knowing that your family trusts you with their deepest thoughts and most difficult challenges, and you will understand where they are coming from.

I know this doesn't happen overnight, but Rome wasn't built in a day either. Step by step, conversation by conversation, if you make the effort to be a careful listener and to actively understand the message behind the words, you will develop the ability to deeply relate to your family . . . and to grow those relationships over time. In this life, it doesn't get better than that.

Give Thanks in All Things

Joe and Sarah had a good marriage and three good kids. Joe travelled a lot and missed a lot of family events, but he was earning good money. At first, when Joe lost his job in a corporate downsizing, the couple didn't worry too much about the future. But as the Great Recession of 2008 set in and Joe couldn't find a new job that paid as much as he had earned previously their worries began to mount. As the For Sale signs in their neighborhood began to accumulate, they realized their house was probably worth less than they had paid for it—a lot less. As the months dragged on, their worries continued to grow. Tempers got short as things got tougher. One day, things reached a boiling point and almost exploded. Joe realized that something had to change or his marriage was in real danger of failing.

Joe sought out some older men in their church—guys he knew a bit and respected a great deal. He sat down with two of them separately and had the courage to be flat-out honest with them. He also sat down with his pastor to talk things over. Out of these honest and heart-felt conversations, Joe realized that he had to make some changes. One of the things he decided to do was to be completely honest with his wife about his fears for the future and his feelings of failure. Just doing that helped Joe and Lisa to restore a spirit of teamwork and friendship that had been missing for a while. He also began to devote himself to prayer much more earnestly, every single day. That also helped in ways big and small. But maybe the most important change Joe realized he had to make was in his own attitude.

Joe realized that for months he had been driven by fear and worry. He knew these negative emotions were not helping him or his family (or his job search) in any way, but he didn't know how to change them. Then an older friend challenged him to "give thanks in all things" according to the biblical injunction found in 1 Thessalonians 5:18. Joe understood that he should give thanks for the good things in life, but he was puzzled when his older friend explained that God wanted him to give Him thanks for *all* things, not just the good stuff. At first this seemed ridiculous to Joe. Why give thanks for getting laid off? Why give thanks for the difficult financial challenges he and his wife now faced? Why give thanks at all?

Joe's older friend then told him some of the most powerful words Joe had ever heard: "because it makes you invincible." Joe didn't understand, so his friend went on to explain, "If we live by fear, we will always be worrying about today or about tomorrow or about something." Joe had to admit that he'd been walking in fear for many months now, and that it had only made things worse. His friend continued, "If we live by faith, we live in the light of the biblical truth that 'in *all* things God works for the good of those who love him' (Romans 8:28, *NIV*, emphasis added). That means we can accept—and thank Him—for even the tough things."

Joe was beginning to see what his friend was driving at. "God doesn't want us, His children, to be emotional infants," his friend said. "He wants us to grow strong in faith and hope and love. And the only way to do that is to grow through the tough things in life—and give thanks for them." Joe was dumbfounded, but he felt a strong, quiet peace in his heart at the same time. "And that's what makes us invincible?" he asked his older friend. "Quite so," replied the older man, "for the joy of the Lord is a man's truest and deepest source of strength, and nothing and no one can ever take it from him."

Most of us guys, if we're deeply honest with ourselves, aren't real strong with the Relational Tools. Some are, but for most of us it's something we need to improve (and that certainly includes me). So do take a good look at the Put It to Work Guide at the end of this chapter, which was designed specifically to help you strengthen and sharpen your Relational Tools. The good news is that these tools will serve you well both with your family (where they are truly vital), with your colleagues at work, and with your friends at the club or at church—in fact, just about everywhere. Life, at its core, is all about relationships, which is why mastering the Relationship Tool is so important. And master it you can.

For Further Reflection

1. On a 1 to 10 scale (with 1 as the best), how would you rate your skills at active listening? Active understanding? Deeply relating?

2. What grades would your family give you on those three? Please ask them. If their scores and your scores differed a lot, why was that? What can you learn from that?

3. Where do you have opportunities to improve your Relationship Tool? How do you plan to do that?

Today's Quick Wins

1. Take 60 seconds to think back to a time when you felt truly and deeply understood and appreciated by someone whose opinion mattered a lot. Remember how good that felt.

2. Take 60 seconds to reflect on how important it is for your family members to feel understood and appreciated by you.

3. Take 60 seconds to envision your family in the future when each member of the family knows deep down that he or she is understood and deeply appreciated for who he or she is.

Your Relationship Toolset

Let's take a look at how we can further develop each of the three primary relational tools we discussed in this chapter. We'll first look at careful listening and see how we can sharpen that important tool in our Relationship Toolset.

The Three Keys to Careful Listening

Careful listening is a skill that can help you in a big way within your family and beyond. You can develop careful listening skills in regular day-to-day interactions with your wife or children's mother, your children and your friends—no special training or practice situations are needed. Mastering the art of careful listening will even help you at work and in every area of your life where human interaction is important. But how exactly do you develop your skills in careful listening? Here are three keys:

1. *Fully tune in to what the speaker is saying.* This will require two types of effort on your part. First, you need to put aside all competitors for your attention—newspaper, cell phone, magazine or whatever else. Second, you need to focus your full attention on the speaker. This will show the person that you value what he or she is saying and that he or she is important to you.

2. *Ask good questions or make appropriate comments when the speaker asks for feedback.* These skills further your understanding while having the added benefit of showing

the speaker that you are truly tuned into what he or she is saying.

3. *Bring the conversation up a few days or weeks later as appropriate.* Your spouse or child (or colleague) will deeply appreciate that you have remembered the conversation and care enough about it to bring it up again.

Mastering the Skill of Active Listening

Mastering the skill of careful listening will help you master the next skill in the Relational Toolset: active understanding. As we discussed in this chapter, active understanding is based on careful listening, because we will never really understand another human being if we haven't listened carefully to him or her over an extended period of time. Most dads I speak with believe they have a pretty good active understanding of their families. In some cases this is true, but in many cases not so much. So here's a little test to see how well you understand them:

1. Write down what you believe are the three biggest worries your wife (or children's mother) has today. Put them in order, starting with what you believe is her biggest worry.

2. Write down what you believe are the three biggest sources of joy in her life today. Put them in order, starting with what you believe is her biggest source of joy.

3. Write down what you believe are the three biggest worries for each of your children. Put them in order, starting with what you believe is each child's biggest worry.

4. Write down what you believe are the three biggest sources of joy in each of your children's lives. Put them in order, starting with what you believe is the biggest source of joy for each child.

5. Talk with each member of your family, starting with
   your wife or children's mother, and see how close your
   answers are to reality. It should be a fun and interesting series of conversations!

If your answers matched up well with your family member's
reality, congratulations! You do, indeed, have a good active understanding of the members of your family. If not, just asking them
and carefully listening to their answers probably furthered your
active understanding of each person, and that is a very good thing.

Relating Deeply to Family Members

Over time, as you practice careful listening and use it to build an
active understanding of each member of your family, you will begin to relate deeply to them. Relating deeply to each member of
your family is not about having similar personalities, political
views or musical tastes (thankfully). In fact, it doesn't depend on
circumstances or external similarities at all. Relating deeply is
more about truly understanding, empathizing and appreciating
the person each one is deep down at the heart level.

Some couples are blessed with an ability to actively understand each other and relate deeply to one another almost right
away. But in my experience, this is quite rare, and even couples that
are blessed in this way must continue to work on careful listening
and active understanding in order to maintain their ability to relate deeply. Why is that? Because people and circumstances change
over time.

For those couples who were not blessed in this way (and that's
the majority of us), we ultimately have a choice. We can choose to
build the deepest possible relationships with our families using
the skills of careful listening, active understanding and relating
deeply; or we can just watch TV or do other things that don't involve our families and continue to relate to them at the surface
level. Frankly, that's the easier choice. But the TV will never listen
to you, or understand you, or relate to you in any meaningful way.

So even though it is the easier path, it is one that eventually leads to emptiness and loneliness.

Do yourself and your family a huge favor: Put your Relational Toolset to work. Practice and improve your careful listening, active understanding and relating deeply tools. You will be forever glad you did.

Three Ways to Strengthen Your Relationship Tools

Finally, here are three ways that you can strengthen your Relational Tools in the next 30 days:

1. *Write your wife or children's mother a long letter, and then write one to each of your children separately.* If your relationship has been rocky or non-existent, be open to admitting that in the letter. Admit your fault in the problem and say that you want to build a better and stronger relationship. Prepare some good questions in advance about things you know are important to the person. For example, you might ask your wife or children's mother about her biggest worry these days, or about specific things you know your child is worried about (grades, friends, finances, getting into college, graduating from college, getting a job, getting braces . . . the potential list is almost endless). Ask her to write back and respond to each question. Think carefully about the responses of your family members, and try to read between the lines and understand their real concerns. Then ask follow-up questions to ensure that you actively understand what you have heard.

2. *A few days after receiving their letters, go back to each family member and follow up on the issues that were shared.* Help your family members see that you really were paying

attention and that as a result you have an active understanding of their concerns. Ask them some good follow-up questions (e.g., "Do you need any help with those job applications?" "Have you thought further about applying to that college?" "Did you ever call Jill and find out what she meant by that remark?"). These questions will help you actively understand how their thinking on these key issues is evolving. And, of course, offer to help in any way you can (e.g., "Hey, the manager of that store is a friend of my good friend Sam's—would you like me to ask Sam to put a good word in for you after your job interview?").

3. *At least once a week after that, be sure to check in with your family members on where they are on the issues they shared with you.* Doing this will help you learn to relate deeply to them by actively understanding the issues that are front and center in their lives. As you learn more about each member of your family, they will (usually) take a greater interest in the pressures, concerns and realities of your life outside the family as well.

Remember that all organizations take on the character of their leader. So, over time, your leadership in your family, using your Relational Toolset, should mean that members of your family will learn to wield their own Relational Tools with greater skill. This will mean better relationships all around—and a stronger family over time.

Seventh Inning Stretch

*A time to pause and reflect on how we are
doing at becoming better dads.*

We're way more than halfway done here. So be honest:
How is it going? I hope and pray that our journey together so far has been fun, inspiring and challenging in
equal parts. I also hope that you will take a moment to share with
me your feedback on the book, the website and/or anything else
you'd like to share. I would deeply appreciate hearing from you at
www.facebook.com/BeaBetterDadToday.

I hope you're not losing steam. If you are, consider taking a
reading break. You could use the time to put some of your newly
sharpened tools in your fatherhood toolset to work. Find out from
your family members about what's working and what isn't. Or just
pray for the guidance to be the best dad you can be. Frankly, those
are all probably more important than reading another chapter of
this book today.

Remember what we discussed at the outset? This is not a
"normal" book. My hope and prayer is that this is not a book that
you just read through and then forget about a few months later.
I hope this is more like a reference book or a training manual for
you—a book that is going to help you become a better dad today . . . and every day going forward for the rest of your life. I hope
it is a book that you read slowly and try to get the most you can
out of every chapter. I also hope it is a book you can go back to
when you need a bit of encouragement or some new ideas on the
fatherhood front.

As I also said at the outset, that's the main reason—in fact, the
only reason—I wrote this book. So if you're getting discouraged, or
you're just tired, or you need some help with a specific issue that

isn't addressed in the book (and, trust me, in any book like this there are lots of issues we just don't have space to get into), please take a few minutes to go to www.facebook.com/BeaBetterDad Today and ask for help. There you will also find a resource we have named "Granddads on Call," a team of experienced fathers and grandfathers who are happy to discuss anything you would like to talk about. (Note: This service does cost a small amount just to help defray our costs to provide the help—otherwise it would quickly cease to exist.)

Remember, fatherhood is meant to be fun. Sure, it's a lot of work, but it is also the best job in the world. And you are, quite literally, the most qualified person in the entire world for that job (at least as far as your own family is concerned). As a matter of fact, you are irreplaceable. So don't get discouraged. As we've said, Rome wasn't built in a day, and neither are world-class fathers. Hang in there. Keep using the Ten Tools of Fatherhood, and over time, you *will* see the fruit of your labor. And that will be a wonderful thing to behold.

So, do take a break from this book if you need one. No worries. But don't take a break from becoming a better dad. After all, if you're a dad now, you will be one for the rest of your life—so why not be the very best dad you can be?

TOOL #7

Heaven's Help

*To be the best earthly father you can be,
you need help from the Ultimate Father.*

I came that they might have life, and have it abundantly.
JOHN 10:10, *NASB*

*I grew up in a totally broken family. My dad was an alcoholic and an
adulterer. But by God's grace—and with His help—my wife and I have four
wonderful kids, aged 10 to 22. And nothing could be better than that.*
DANIEL S., NEW YORK, NEW YORK

If you would like to discuss any of this material via email,
feel free to contact me at **gws@beabetterdadtoday.com**

After reading the title of this chapter, you might be saying to yourself, *Yes, of course I need God's help.* Or perhaps you are asking yourself, *What the heck does he mean by "Heaven's Help"?* No matter what your reaction to this chapter's title, I hope that you will hang with me here. Hear me out at least by reading the whole chapter. Then, if you want to dismiss these ideas, at least you will have heard me out.

The title of this section means something very simple: Are you willing to ask God Almighty to help you be a better dad? You and I might have a different understanding of God and how to do that, and that's okay. I'm not claiming some kind of divine mandate on my understanding of God—and I'll bet you're not either—but one thing I'm sure we both agree on is that we could use some heavenly help on this fatherhood thing. Here's the good news: The Bible portrays God in many ways. But one of the many amazing things about the New Testament is how Jesus teaches us (many times) that God is our heavenly Father. Unless you're a scholar of comparative religions, you might not immediately grasp how revolutionary this was . . . and is.

Two thousand years ago, most human beings worshiped a wide variety of local and regional idols. Think of the old Greek and Roman gods like Zeus or Neptune, which still have a (small) place in modern memory. These gods were capricious, unreliable and competitive with each other. Many had to be appeased with human sacrifices. And none, absolutely none, was portrayed as being our "heavenly Father."

Some people decry the God of Israel as portrayed in the Old Testament as some vengeful deity who smote people right and left. But a careful analysis will reveal a very different picture. Throughout the entire Old Testament, one theme rings true again and again, and it is the message of the very first of the 10 Commandments: "I am the LORD your God who brought you out of the land of Egypt, out of the house of slavery. You shall have no other gods before Me" (Deuteronomy 5:6-7, *NASB*). Throughout the Old Testament it seems that God was preparing the people of Israel to be the world's first consistently monotheistic people.

Finally, after many missteps, lost opportunities and even exiles, Israel got the message.

That set the stage for Jesus' truly radical teachings . . . and the New Testament. Jesus taught things that were truly radical for His day (or any day). Love for our enemies, the power of servant leadership, the separation of church and state . . . and the ultimate truth: that we have a heavenly Father who loves us and has provided a way for us to have a relationship with Him as His beloved children. That love doesn't depend on our looks, our wealth or our family connections, and it doesn't depend on how much we do for Him or sacrifice to Him—as the old pagan gods used to demand. His love is there for each of us just because He loves us. As the old saying goes, "We are engraved on the palm of His hand."

Think about it: If Jesus had shown up in a polytheistic culture (that is to say, a place where many different gods were worshiped), He would have been just one god among many. Interesting teachings, sure. But, hey, just one more god to add to the list of gods we worship around here. No big deal. Instead, Jesus showed up in Israel, the only monotheistic society in the world at the time, and claimed to be the only Son of the only God who was, in fact, the heavenly Father of us all. That was so radical that the religious and political leaders of the time conspired to put Him to death. But remember, without the prep work done in the Old Testament to help Israel become the world's first consistently monotheistic culture, none of it would have mattered.

The Great Revelation of Scripture

Today, the large majority of human beings belong to a very small number of faith traditions. For the atheist, it is very hard to explain how the "illegitimate" son of an itinerant carpenter who was executed as a criminal is now the head of the world's largest religion: Christianity. The fact that more than over two billion people on earth today are Christians in one form or another is very hard to explain apart from a supernatural power. The fact that the second largest faith tradition (Islam) also springs from Old

Testament roots—and acknowledges Jesus as the "Christ" and "the foremost of God's prophets"—is also a tricky "coincidence" for your typical atheist. And the fact that the oldest of the world's major monotheistic religions (Judaism) is the faith from which both Christianity and Islam springs . . . well, that is another unanswerable puzzle for the atheist believer.

My point here is not to bash atheists, for whom I actually have a great deal of intellectual respect. To be a sincere atheist is a tremendous leap of faith (which is why I use the term "atheist believer"). In fact, it is at least as great a leap of faith as the one I made in becoming a Christian in my senior year at Dartmouth College. And whereas my leap of faith has resulted in many years of (sometimes difficult) personal growth in love and hope and joy, the leap of faith of the sincere atheist lands him in a world where nothing really matters. Nothing. Because if you believe that we are just atoms that happened to come together when we are born and then come apart when we die, there can be no truth. No God. No soul. No right. No wrong. The law of the jungle is ultimately the only law, because the strongest makes the rules . . . whatever they are. Yes, I have a great deal of respect for all sincere atheists. They have a certain strength of character that I lack. In a world like that, I would rather not live.

Fortunately, the teaching of the Old and New Testaments leads to this great revelation: You and I both have a heavenly Father who loves us—and all people—as His very own children. As John 1:12 states, "Yet to all who received [Christ], to those who believed in his name, he gave the right to become children of God." That means that our life does have meaning—and that there can be a true right and wrong. It means that we must respect and honor all men and women as God's children. It means that this life on earth is not the end of the story. In fact, this life on earth is just a short introduction to a much more beautiful story to come.

It also means that our heavenly Father can understand what it means to be a dad, for He Himself has a Son. That Son, in turn, can fully identify with our weaknesses and the difficulties of our lives. In fact, He died to break the power of sin and death in our lives.

And when He rose from the grave (the proof that the power of sin and death had been defeated), He left us His Holy Spirit to help us to be better people, better men, better fathers. This truly is good news—and it has many positive implications for our lives. But when it comes to being a better dad, it means three main things:

1. *God loves us each as individuals,* not in some mystical far-off way, but in a real, personal way. He wants to help us be the best men—and the best fathers—we can be. We just have to ask for His help—and let Him help us (which we do when we walk by faith).

2. *Just as Jesus completed His earthly mission, so too He wants to help us complete our earthly mission,* a big part of which is to be the best fathers we can be. He wants to hear (and to answer) our prayers for our families. But we have to be willing to trust Him with our prayers . . . and our lives.

3. *Jesus did not leave us alone to accomplish that task, but left us His Holy Spirit* to help us move forward. The Holy Spirit can watch after our kids—and help them—in ways that we as parents simply cannot. But He will only do that *if* we commit them (and ourselves) to His love and care.

I'm sure you can see right away how important—and how powerful—these truths are for us as fathers, if we understand them and take advantage of them. But that's a big IF.

The Challenge that Lies Before Us

I know that someone reading this book may just flat-out not believe these things. I also know that some struggle to believe them. For one-third of my life I didn't believe these things at all, and for other parts of my life I have struggled with them. But now I know them to be true; for me they have been the fuel my soul needed when my earthly tank ran dry; the soothing balm for my heart when I needed grace; the supernatural wisdom for my life when I needed understanding. I cannot prove them to you. All I suggest is that you check it out for yourself. I'm not telling you what to believe. You have to figure that out for yourself . . . we all do. But I am telling you that it is very possible that it is true. So isn't it worth finding out for yourself?

One of the best ways to start is with a simple, heartfelt prayer for help. That's how my whole faith journey began many years ago. If God is who Jews and Christians have believed Him to be for more than 3,000 years—which is pretty much all of recorded human history—He will answer. Not only does He love you, but also you and He have something really important in common: you are both dads. He wants to help you to be the very best dad you can be.

However, in order to see the answer to your prayers, you have to be asking sincerely, listening humbly and watching carefully, because He answers in His own way and in His own time. But answer He will. Check it out for yourself.

For those of us who know the love of God in our hearts and lives, the question is this: Are we going forward with Him? The life of faith is like riding a bicycle: Either you are making progress and going forward, or you are about to fall off. There is no standing still. This is one place the American Church has largely failed its men in the last 50 years. By and large, the Church has not challenged enough of its men to go onward and upward in the maturity, wisdom, love and joy of Christ.

Too many pastors and priests—and too many Christian men—are content to go to church once in a while, put a few bucks in the offering plate, and not kill anyone. Unfortunately for these men, they are missing out on perhaps life's most exciting journey—the journey of becoming the very best men they can be through God's help.

That is the challenge that lies before each and every one of us. So ask yourself: *Do I truly want to be the very best man I can be? Do I want to become the best father, the best husband and the best friend I can be?* If so, you are going to need God's help, for that is not something you can do on your own. So take time to kneel down right where you are, right now, and ask for His help. Don't be ashamed, for the strongest man is the one who can kneel down before the King of kings. He *will* help you—of that you can be sure.

Defeating the Power of Sin

A word from our brother in the faith, the writer of the New Testament letter to the Hebrews in Rome, helps us put this battle in perspective. We are not on our own. Many great fathers have gone before us, and this great passage reminds us that we are not alone: "Therefore, since we are surrounded by such a great cloud of witnesses, let us throw off everything that hinders and the sin that so easily entangles, and let us run with perseverance the race that is marked out for us" (Hebrews 12:1, *NIV*). Do you have a besetting sin that is hindering you from going forward to become a better man? Maybe it's your temper, or your wandering eye or your penny-pinching spirit. Or maybe you drink a bit too much or are addicted to something, or have made your job/bank account/career an idol in your life. Or maybe you've grown angry or bitter over time and have shut God out of your life—or just kept Him as a decorative ornament on the outside, but without any real connection on the inside.

Whatever the besetting sin, brother, I have four words for you: Welcome to the Club! The truth is this: We all have one or more challenges like these in our lives. And we have two choices: (1) We can either allow them to grow and master us, or (2) we can grow to master them. That's it. There is no middle ground. As we discussed previously, the spiritual life is binary. We are either moving forward or we are moving backward. So let's move forward.

How do you do that? An excellent question, and one that we can only briefly touch on here. But there are some great books on this subject that I highly recommend. Here are three:

1. *Experiencing God*, by Henry Blackaby, Richard Blackaby and Claude King. This is probably my favorite Christian book of all time.

2. *Counterfeit Gods: The Empty Promises of Money, Sex, and Power, and the Only Hope that Matters* by Timothy Keller. Another fabulous work by one of the greatest preachers of our generation.

3. *Victory Over the Darkness,* by Neil T. Anderson.

If you are seeking to live a victorious life by defeating the power of sin in your heart, here are three important suggestions:

1. *Be totally honest with God, confess your sin and ask Him sincerely for His help.* I know this sounds basic, and it is. But the road to victory starts with the first step. And this is it.

2. *Share your struggle with your pastor, rabbi, church elder, chaplain or priest.* These spiritual professionals, as long as they are true men of faith who love God and honor His Word, should be able to help you in your battle. Think of your pastor or priest or rabbi as a spiritual mentor, because that's what he can be for you. He can help you understand yourself better and give you the spiritual guidance and support you need to win the battle.

3. *Confide in a close (and mature) Christian brother or brothers and ask for their prayers, support and help in holding you accountable.* True friendship is having a couple of close friends who know your struggles, pray for you daily and hold you accountable to the standards you know are right and good. We all need a few good and true friends.

Each of these steps will shed light and help you to be victorious in the particular struggle you face today, for it will reveal the sin that is hidden in your heart. Sin loves the shadows and the darkness—and it especially loves any phoniness it can find in your life, because hypocrisy creates darkness in our souls. In fact, sin is very much like an infection: If you keep it in the dark and don't clean it up or expose it to salt and light (both disinfectants and both terms that Jesus used to describe healthy Christians), it almost always gets worse. But if you bring it out into the open, cleanse the infection and keep it clean, it loses its power over you and, little by little, gets healed. That's why it is so important to be honest and accountable before God, before your spiritual mentor(s) and before your closest friends. It is in that process that you will receive the help you need to defang the power of sin in your life. No doubt this will not be an easy process (it's not), and no doubt it will require discipline and diligence on your part (it will).

By getting God's help and the help of others to master your sinful nature, you will allow your spiritual nature to grow more and more in the love and joy and peace and wisdom that Christ promised all who follow Him. Just as Jesus pictured in His famous "I am the vine, you are the branches" teaching in John 15, you must be vitally and truthfully connected to Him in order to grow. And to do that, you simply must get rid of the sin that "so easily entangles" like a weed, choking off the True Vine.

As the spiritual leader of your family, you can be sure of one thing: If you are not growing in the love and joy and peace and wisdom of God (as He promises to all believers), then your family is not growing as much as they could be in these good fruits either. And don't you want your family to see the fruit of the Spirit (see Galatians 5:22-23) in their own lives? Remember, if you are not a good spiritual leader for your household, you and your family are missing out on some of life's richest blessings.

You can do it—and you can help your family walk on the path of robust spiritual growth as well. Remember one of the greatest promises of Scripture: "The prayer of a righteous man is powerful and effective" (James 5:16, NIV). The promise is not just for some men, at some time, but for all men . . . always. The best news about that promise is this: As Christians, we know that our righteousness is found in Christ. He is our righteousness. So that promise is for all of us who want to put it into practice by praying diligently for our families.

The Importance of a Dad's Spiritual Leadership

My friend Randy, with the partnership of his lovely wife, has done a great job of providing strong spiritual support for their three girls. Early in their marriage they found a great church where the girls could make young friends, with whom they have now grown up. They try to have a deep discussion once or twice a week at the dinner table about right and wrong, usually in the context of some piece of local or national news. Both Randy and his wife take each girl out separately at least once a month to talk with her about what's going on in her life, the challenges she is facing and so forth. The girls have matured through all of this—and each of them is now a wonderful, well-adjusted and successful young adult. The older two are both dating young men who themselves are strong, courageous men of faith (much like my friend Randy). He has seen the promise of God's Word come to pass: "Train up a child in the way he should go, and when he is old he will not turn from it" (Proverbs 22:6, *NIV*).

The Importance of Praying for Your Family

I cannot emphasize enough the importance of praying diligently and sincerely for your family. I do not pretend to understand exactly how prayer works, but I have seen the power of prayer change hearts (first and foremost, my own) and circumstances. It is by earnest, heartfelt prayer that we link arms, so to speak, with our almighty Father.

For some reason that I can only partially grasp, God often waits for our prayers before He moves in ways both big and small. Maybe it is because He wants us to grow in faith. Maybe it is because He just enjoys fellowship with us through prayer. Whatever the reason, prayer is critical if we desire heaven's help for ourselves and our families. Let me give you one of many examples of this from my own family.

A number of years back, one of our children was getting sucked into something that was definitely not good. My wife and I were getting more and more concerned, but at the same time, we were young parents and tried to put a brave face on it (after all, who wants to admit that their kid is in trouble?). Finally, we realized that we had neglected one of our strongest potential weapons on behalf of our child, and we began to pray diligently about the situation. We asked God to show us the magnitude of the problem and help us deal with it wisely, lovingly and effectively, no matter how big it was.

What followed was a minor miracle. For some reason that I will never be able to explain, one night as my wife and I were praying about this issue, I just felt "led" to go look into our outside trash cans. I have never done that before—or since. But that one night, close to the top of one of our trash cans, was proof positive that our child had a serious problem that had to be confronted. To say that the whole thing amazed me would be an understatement. It was a miraculous answer to prayer—pure and simple.

So we prayed about how to confront our child in love and truth (the two always have to go together, as we discussed in Tool #3, "True Moral Compass and True Humility"). We used the "revelation" that I had found in the garbage to confront and show our child that what was going on mattered to us a lot—and even mattered to God. Our child knew that I never went through the garbage, so it certainly got our child's attention that the one night that child put something incriminating in the trash was the very same night that God, through His Holy Spirit, moved me to check the garbage cans.

The fact that we cared enough to talk directly and lovingly about this issue helped our child a lot. That evening, the three of us cried together—and I think our child understood how worried we were and how much that child was loved. I can't tell you that we won the battle that evening, or even that month or that year. We even decided to move to another state to help remove our child from that very negative influence. But today that child (and, by God's grace, each of our kids) is doing well—and is free and clear of that destructive sin.

Again, I am not saying that we saw an overnight miracle or a sudden and complete change (although those things can and do happen through prayer—I have seen it a few times myself). But I am saying that over time, with the prayer support of a number of dear friends and the constant love and support of the whole family, our child turned away from that destructive behavior. Prayer was a key part of that battle. Without it, I think the outcome might have been very different.

Exercising your spiritual leadership on behalf of your family is not easy, but it sure beats the alternative. And it starts with the heart of the leader . . . you. If you are a Christian man, spiritual growth is not optional. I have said it before, but it is well worth repeating: Either you are moving forward in the Christian life, growing in love and peace and joy and wisdom, or you are going backward—there is no standing still. So let's move forward. Not only will we benefit personally, but our family will benefit greatly as well.

Beware the Attacks of the Father of Lies

At this point, I want to talk about something that many today dismiss as "unscientific" or "old-fashioned," because you need to be prepared for challenges that will arise as you start moving ahead spiritually. The Bible could not be clearer about the fact that God exists and is at work in our world through His Holy Spirit. But the Bible is also clear that there is an evil one at work in our world, and that he operates through lies, deception, hatred and sin. Yes, you heard me correctly: The devil really does exist.

Although I had never even heard the term until I was in my twenties, I have come to see over the past 20-plus years that spiritual warfare is real—and we as fathers must take an active stand on that spiritual battlefront (which is another important reason to pray diligently for our families, friends, nation and world). Sometimes the evil one's work is clearly seen in the self-destructive nature of addiction or the self-delusional ranting of a serial killer. Looking back in history, we can see some clear examples of the evil one's work on a macro-scale. For example, Hitler's use of critically needed men and material to build a Europe-wide network of extermination camps to kill six million Jewish people (and millions of other people groups he didn't like) was motivated by something very different than military strategy or self-interest. In fact, Hitler's increasing devotion to what he called "the final solution" (the elimination of the Jewish race) almost certainly accelerated the defeat of the Third Reich by the Allies. It is clear that Hitler was motivated by other, even darker sources.

Many of us in the West don't pay much attention to spiritual warfare today. Interestingly enough, in cultures that are more accepting of the spiritual dimension of life, from Southeast Asia to South America to Africa, evidence of spiritual warfare is sometimes much clearer and much easier to see. Having lived almost half of my adult life in these regions of the world, I have seen with my own eyes some things that were impossible to explain except as spiritual phenomena.

But here in the West, more often than not, the evil one works through subtle lies or self-delusions that lead us (gently) down the wrong path: "You've had a tough day; it's okay to [drink too much, check out some Internet porn, or whatever]." Or maybe he says, "Your wife doesn't really understand you, and [Miss XXX] is so fun just to talk with." Or maybe he whispers, "Your life would really be great if you could just close this deal, so it's okay to [cheat or lie or exaggerate or whatever]."

You know what I'm talking about. Those little lies can be very powerful and very tempting. But remember, no man ever set out to ruin his future and his family via addiction, adultery or fraud. It came upon him little by little until he was firmly hooked. From there, all the evil one had to do was reel him in.

Let's face it: The father of lies doesn't really worry about the folks who are in his camp already. He's got them on the line (so to speak); he just needs to reel them in over the course of time. And he's got a lifetime to do it. But he gets angry—and tries to get active—in the lives of those who are working to bring light and life and love into this world. Your family is not at all off limits. In fact, they are prime targets.

The growth of good fruit in your life and in the lives of those around you (which the Bible defines as love, joy, peace, patience, goodness, gentleness, faithfulness and self-control) is indisputable evidence of spiritual progress. One of the other ways that you can know you are making spiritual progress is when you start to face more spiritual opposition. But not to worry. As the Bible promises us, "He who is in you is greater than he who is in the world" (1 John 4:4). God, whose Holy Spirit is with you, is much more powerful than the evil one who seeks to destroy you. He will show you the way, as long as you are walking with Him.

Help for Your Fatherhood Journey

This has been a long chapter, but it is vital to your development as a father. None of us had a perfect earthly father—and some of us had no earthly father at all. But each of us has a powerful and loving heavenly Father who wants to help us be the very best dads we can be. Not only did He give us real, tangible evidence of that love in the person of His Son, Jesus Christ, but He also sent His Holy Spirit to help us today to be the best men, and the best fathers, we can be.

Please meditate on that fact and really let it sink in. It is amazing, but it is also true. You have a heavenly Father who loves you— truly and sincerely loves you. Even though He knows you down to your innermost core and knows all of the junk that is down there, He still loves you. He knows everything that you have ever done—the good, the bad and the ugly. He knows you and He loves you so much that He forgives you for the sake of His Son.

Yes, God is a Father too, and He loves you as a son for the sake of His Son, Jesus. But He hasn't just left you alone on this earth. He has sent His own Spirit to help you grow in the fruits of the Spirit, day by day. As His Word promises, He will produce the fruit of love, joy, peace, patience, kindness, goodness, faithfulness, gentleness and self-control in our lives. That's exactly the type of good fruit each of us needs as fathers for our families.

Don't believe me? Of course I cannot convince you; you have to make this decision on your own. But I do urge you to check it out for yourself. If you do that with a sincere and humble heart, I believe strongly that He will answer you. He will do that because He loves you. He truly does want to help you to be the very best earthly father you can be.

For Further Reflection

1. What do you really believe about God? Have you ever sincerely asked the Lord to reveal Himself to you? Why or why not?

2. Why do you think Jesus introduced the world to the concept of "God the Father"?

3. What, if any, sins are keeping you from growing as a man, as a father and as a Christian? Do you have the courage to confess those sins to God in prayer and turn away from them? Why or why not?

Today's Quick Wins

1. Take 60 seconds to meditate on the fact that you have a heavenly Father who truly loves you. (Even if you don't believe that, please set your unbelief aside for 60 seconds to contemplate the possible reality of being fully loved by a heavenly Father who knows you completely.)

2. Take 60 seconds to reflect on how much God the Father loves His own Son—and, therefore, how well He understands our trials and tribulations as dads.

3. Take 60 seconds to sincerely and humbly ask Him to help you become the very best dad you can be. Over time, He will.

Getting Help from Your Heavenly Father

This is a harder Put It to Work section to write simply because each of us is in a different place in our spiritual journey. Some of us enjoy close fellowship with our heavenly Father as we walk with Him day by day. Some of us are Christians, but we'd like to more fully experience the love and joy and peace that Christ promises to all who walk closely with Him. Some of us are not sure where we are on the spiritual front. And some of us are members of other faiths or have little or no faith at all. However, wherever you are today, it is important that you recognize that you are on a spiritual journey—even if you don't fully understand it yet.

To make this section as helpful as possible, I've written a separate Put It to Work Guide for each of these above groups. For this reason, feel free to skip to the section that best describes your own spiritual state today. Of course, you're free to read the other ones (in fact, I hope you will), but you might want to focus on the one that is closest to where you feel you are right now. Hopefully, it will be an encouragement and even a blessing to you today.

For Those Who Are Walking Closely with Christ or Would Like to Walk More Closely with Him

Thank you for taking a stand for righteousness and truth. Thank you for committing your life to the power of faith, hope and love. Thank you for your desire to be the very best father, husband, neighbor, co-worker and friend you can be. Because if you are truly walking with Jesus Christ every day, that is what you are called to be doing.

The big question for guys like us is this: Are we continuing to grow and develop in the faith, or have we stalled out? Undoubtedly, you already know the truth of Jesus' statement, "to whom much was given, of him much will be required" (Luke 12:48, *ESV*). The truth is that if you are a follower of Jesus Christ, you have a big head start on being a really good dad (or at least you should have). God's love and His truth are twin towers of strength and wisdom for us. But, like any gift, it's up to us to open them up and put them to work in our lives. I pray that this book has been helping you do just that and that www.FellowshipOfFathers.com will help you to find the tools, services and encouragement to continue your ongoing progress as a father, a husband and a man of God.

So, here is my basic challenge to you as a man of faith: *Are you growing in faith and hope and love, or are you stalled?* The only certain evidence of spiritual life is spiritual growth. Just like an airplane, we are either moving forward or we are stalling. The stall won't last long if not corrected; it will go from stall to fall all too quickly.

The trouble is that it is easy for us as Christians to rely on a distant historical experience, or the fact that we go to church, or the fact that we have the "right" beliefs about God or any number of other "facts." Don't get me wrong; none of these things are bad. But they can all be substitutes for what the Lord really wants from us, which is our sincere friendship, our heartfelt love and our faithful obedience.

Look back at the book of Genesis before the Fall. What is the picture we see of Adam? Was Adam a man who constantly pointed back to some historic "born again" experience many years previous? No. Was he a man who went to church? No. Was he a man who was proud of having the right beliefs about God? No.

Again, none of these things are bad (unless we make them idols or substitutes for a true relationship with God). It is that Father/son love relationship with God that matters more than anything else. Again, look at Adam. He had his day job (master gardener) and his lifetime calling ("be fruitful and multiply" [Genesis 1:28, *NASB*])—which meant taking care of his wife, Eve, and creating a strong and loving family with her. But most importantly, he had what appears to be a vibrant and deep relationship with God (look at how they walked together "in the cool of the day" [Genesis 3:8, *NASB*]).

Of course, sin ruined all that—as unchecked sin will do for any of us today. But the point is that the God of the Universe created Adam and Eve to have fellowship with Him—which is amazing. What is even more amazing is that He wants to have that same type of loving, heartfelt friendship with you (and me) today. He does not want us to wallow in our sin but receive the victory He has given us over sin. I know it is hard to believe. But that, in a nutshell, is the overarching message of the Bible: God Almighty seeking to show us His love for humanity (and for us as individuals)—and hoping that we will respond in kind.

So that is my question for you, brother: How is your love relationship with Jesus today? Is it strong and growing? Or is it a bit stagnant and maybe even stalled? Or is it in free fall? Only you know the true answer to that question. You know it right now in your heart. And that is *the* most important question of your life, because everything else in your life ultimately depends on it.

The truth is that we all need help at times. We all grow weary or weak or discouraged. We all fail at times. All of us. So how does God make us into the overcoming champions, the mature men of faith and hope and love that He wants us to be? He gives us the strength to get up again and go on with Him.

Brother, if your heart isn't where you know it should be with the Lord today, then take time right now to get off by yourself in a quiet place with Him and get it right. There is nothing more important than this. His grace is sufficient, which is why Jesus came to earth. All you have to do is be honest with Him and ask humbly for His help. He will meet you, because He still wants to walk with you in the cool of the evening just as He did with Adam. Then be sure to stay in close touch with Him. It took me many, many years to develop the discipline of making time to meet with Him daily—just Him and me— to confess my sin and to get my heart cleaned up, get His perspective on the day ahead, and make sure my attitude and priorities were in line with His. There is literally nothing more important in life.

But we as Christian men also need other men of God to help encourage us and spur us on. The author of Hebrews knew that when he encouraged Christians not to stop meeting together but to encourage one another to love and do good works (see Hebrews 10:24-25). If you don't have at least two good Christian brothers in your life, you are a sitting duck for the enemy (aka, Satan, or the Father of Lies). Don't kid yourself; the devil is out there and looking to destroy you, your family and everything good in this world. So find some sincere, strong men of faith and get into some good fellowship. The old biblical truth "a cord of three strands is not quickly broken" (Ecclesiastes 4:12, *NIV*) is still true today. Every single one of us needs strong and faithful friends.

Finally, let's be diligent about our thought life. That is where the battle is always won or lost. If we can remain in touch with God's Spirit through the day, even in the toughest of circumstances, we will be growing in the faith and hope and love of the Lord. Jesus even promises this in John 15 when He tells us that if we remain closely and rightly related to Him, we will continue to grow and "bear much fruit" (verse 5, *NIV*). This sounds hard to do each and every day. But if we start the day out right with Him, asking the Spirit's help to go through the day and walking step by step with Him, and consciously checking in with Him via prayer throughout the day, He will walk with us on that day's journey. Just like a child who is learning to walk, we will get stronger and more able every day. Yes, we will fall, just like the child will, but eventually we will be able to walk through life and not grow weary, to go through life's challenges and not grow faint (as God's Word promises in Isaiah 40:29-31). Check it out, brother—you will see.

For Those Who Are Not Sure Where They Are Spiritually

Let me start by saying thank you for checking out this chapter and this Put It to Work Guide. That took some courage, my friend, and as men we need courage. For the first 21 years of my life, I did not really know what it was to walk with Christ. For some of those years, I was an admirer, certainly. For some, I was a profound skeptic and even an antagonistic enemy. And for others, I would even say I was a quasi-believer. But it was in my senior year at Dartmouth that I finally humbled my own pride (not easy then, and still not easy today) and asked Christ to forgive my sins and walk the road of life with me as my Lord and Savior. And He did. Just like a baby learning to walk, it took me a long time to learn—far longer than it should have—and I still have much to learn today. But that step of faith was by far the most important decision I have ever made. It literally changed my life . . . for the better.

That step of faith is one that no one else can make for you. No one. It doesn't matter if you were baptized as an infant, if you go to church every Sunday, if you sing in the choir, if you have a wonderful believing wife, or all of the above. You still have to make that most fundamental decision: Will you accept the Lordship of Christ in your own heart and life and walk with Him as your Guide on the road of life . . . or not? That is a question worth wrestling with.

Wrestling with the Ultimate Question

I will never forget hitchhiking across the U.S. many years ago with my buddy Ken. As you might remember from an earlier story, Ken was a Christ-follower from a strong Christian family, and one of my best friends. The family's commitment to God and their love for each other had already deeply impressed me.

When Ken and I were in college, we decided to hitchhike across the U.S. one summer (bad idea then; crazy idea now). We actually had a lot of fun, and I will never forget all the deep philosophical discussions Ken and I had along the way. And because they were deep—and they were real—they included the question of God's existence, why we were on this earth, and the meaning of life. I was proud of being an Ivy League agnostic (maybe even an atheist at that point), and I forcefully argued that point of view. Ken, of course, took the other perspective, but always in love and friendship.

One night in Wyoming, near a big lake in the middle of nowhere, we had an especially good discussion late into the evening.

When Ken finally tucked into his sleeping bag, I was left wondering if what he was saying might actually be true. I had to admit that it would be a wonderful thing if it was, but it seemed to me to be extremely unlikely (to put it mildly).

Fortunately, Ken had made me a very reasonable challenge that evening before turning in. He said, "Why don't you check it out for yourself?" He had a point: I certainly had nothing to lose. So that night, as I looked out on the full moon and that beautiful lake, I said a halting, uncertain prayer of sorts. First, I admitted the truth, namely that I had no idea at all if God really existed or not. Then I asked God (if He existed) to please show me if He was real—and to show me the right way to get properly related to Him. I knew in my heart of hearts that if He was real—and if He was the God of the Bible as Ken believed—I would have to make some changes in my life. But that was okay; I really just wanted to know the truth.

That fall, I went back to Dartmouth for my senior year. I made it a point to study the Torah, the Koran, the Buddhist and Hindu scriptures, as well as the Bible. All were pretty foreign to me—and all had some very interesting and helpful points. But little by little, through those studies and also through the love and kindness of a number of Christian students at Dartmouth, I came to see that God was real and that Jesus was simply who He said He was. It didn't come in a blinding flash or revelation; it was more of a slow process over time. On Easter Sunday 1981, I publically accepted Jesus Christ as my Lord and Savior. A month or two later, I was baptized. That was more than 30 years ago—and that was the single best decision I have ever made in my entire life. So here's my challenge to you: Why don't you check it out for yourself?

The existence of God, and what it means for you personally, is a question worth wrestling with. Great men down through the ages—from Martin Luther (one of the founding fathers of the Reformation) to the great French mathematician and philosopher Blaise Pascal; from William Wilberforce (who led the coalition to abolish the British Slave Trade) to George Washington; from Abraham Lincoln to Dr. Martin Luther King, Jr., to name just a few—all wrestled with that question. I hope you will too.

For Those Who Come from Another Faith Tradition . . . or No Faith at All

Of course, there are good dads (and lousy dads) from every faith tradition. I do think that some of the major world faiths (Buddhism, Christianity, Hinduism, Islam and Judaism) provide far stronger fatherhood platforms than others. But you did not choose the faith tradition (or the lack thereof) into which you were born. And God knows that.

I believe that no matter what your faith tradition was or is in your family, the Ten Tools of Fatherhood will help you be a much better dad as you come to master them. And I hope you will put me to the test on this.

Here is my challenge for you: If I am right about who Jesus is—the earthly shape of our heavenly Father—that must mean that He still wants to walk with us today. It must mean that He wants to help each of us be stronger men, better fathers, and more loving husbands . . . no matter what faith tradition we come from. In other words, if Jesus is who He said He was, He loves us and wants to help us be the best men we can be regardless of whether we were born a Christian, a Jew, a Muslim, a Hindu or a Buddhist (or a Sikh, a Jain, a Unitarian, an animist or anything else for that matter).

I admit that I cannot prove these things irrefutably—just as the atheist cannot prove the contrary. That is why it is called faith. But *if* I am right, it means that you can tap into His power and His wisdom and His love regardless of the faith tradition into which you were born. And doesn't that make sense? Wouldn't our heavenly Father want each of us, His sons, to be the best husbands and fathers and men we can be? Of course He would.

Again, I cannot prove this. But no one can disprove it, either. This is one of life's great questions—and it is a question that only you can answer for yourself. It is a question that is truly worth asking. Every single one of us, regardless of our faith tradition, needs help to be the best father and husband we can be . . . and the best men we can be. I believe that our heavenly Father wants to help each of us—and that is why He came Himself into our world in the person of Jesus Christ and why He still is at work in our world today through the Holy Spirit.

So, just as Philip said to his fellow Jews, "Come and see for yourself" (John 1:46, *NLT*). Philip didn't stop being Jewish, and you don't have to stop being whatever you are. Just come and see for yourself. Humble your heart—and allow Him to help you today. Check it out for yourself. In the Bible, the Lord promises that if you ask and continue to ask . . . if you seek and continue to seek . . . if you knock and continue to knock . . . you will find the truth, and the truth will set you free (see Matthew 7:7-8; John 8:32). So check it out, sincerely and truthfully, for yourself. What do you have to lose?

TOOL #8

Other Good Dads

*There are no successful Lone Ranger dads—
you need the support of friends and older role
models from whom you can learn.*

---

*I thought I was the greatest. I didn't have anyone in my life to
tell me otherwise, in part because I wasn't willing to hear the truth
from my wife. Now I see what a jerk I was, but it's too late.*

JACK W., SOON TO BE DIVORCED
LONE RANGER DAD OF TWO

*It's great to have the help, the encouragement and the fellowship of other
men who want to be the best dads they can be. It makes all the difference.*

JEFF R., STAMFORD, CONNECTICUT

If you would like to discuss any of this material via email,
feel free to contact me at **gws@beabetterdadtoday.com**

Regardless of whether or not you agree on Tool #7, "Heaven's Help," I hope that you can heartily agree on the importance of Tool #8, "Other Good Dads." If you do not, I can only assume that you have not been a father for very long. This is because all great fathers, the world over, need to have help from a variety of sources to be good fathers. Extended family, close friends, spiritual mentors, even business colleagues can all be sources of important help at critical times.

There are no great "Lone Ranger" dads. I've never met even one in any culture, and I don't think they exist. Don't get me wrong; I am not saying that we as dads need to all be extroverts who are always asking for help. Not at all. Good dads come in all shapes and sizes and in all temperaments and outlooks on life. But all of the good dads I have ever met—from the heat of Africa to the heart of Paris and from the beauty of Bermuda to the business centers of Beijing—have had the help of others. Do you agree with me on that point?

Just to be sure, let's take a moment to look at why it might be true. Have you ever thought about why even the best baseball players coming out of college are sent to the minor leagues for at least a few years before they get to play in the Majors? It's true. Less than 1 percent of college baseball players go straight to the Major League. One of the reasons for this is so they can get help perfecting their skills from those who have gone before. In fact, the process doesn't end there. Even the best Major Leaguers continue to get coaching throughout their careers. They know that they can always refine their skills, so they seek out those who have gone before to help them do just that.

It's the same with major league dads. We need other good dads around us to encourage us, show us the ropes and help us when we get into a slump or a serious problem. That's not just true for some of us. I strongly believe that it is true for all of us, or at least for all of us who hope to be major league dads someday soon. So, how can you start that process?

How to Be a Major League Dad

Just like the aspiring Major Leaguer, you need to start with an assessment of your current "team" of friends. Are the guys you spend your free time with caring and committed dads? Or, if you are really honest with yourself, are they at the other end of the scale? Or perhaps your friends are a mixed bag. But just like the aspiring Major Leaguer needs the finest coaching and the best teammates he can find to be successful, you need a strong team of friends who will help you become the best dad you can be.

I'm not saying you should throw your old friends under the bus. Good friends are wonderful and valuable, no matter what. But I am saying that if you've spent all your time with guys who don't have families, or who don't care about their families, then you need to change that going forward. We all need positive and productive friends who understand who we are and where we are trying to go . . . and have the courage to help us when we need it.

I have been deeply blessed by a small number of wonderful friends over the years. They are as close to me (and sometimes closer) than my own brother, Marshall, who is himself a great guy and a great dad. These friends know me intimately, encourage me frequently, and are there to help me when I get off track or am feeling down in the dumps (which does happen). Without these brothers, I would not be the man I am today. That's why this book is dedicated, in part, to them.

Perhaps you do not have any close friends. If so, you are not alone—recent research published in the *American Sociological Review* has shown that fully 25 percent of Americans have no close friends, and this is far more likely to be true for men than for women. For those Americans who report having close friendships, the average number of these types of friends has gone down from three, two decades ago, to two today.[1] This is a dangerous social trend for our families, our society and ourselves. Why? Because we were created for relationships—we were never meant to be alone.

Did you ever build a bonfire at the beach? Our family loves doing that together when we can. But have you ever noticed what happens when you take one burning stick out of the bonfire and put it by itself on the sand? It quickly goes out. That's a pretty good example of what happens when you try to be a Lone Ranger dad. The cold realities of life can quickly extinguish your passion to be the best dad you can be.

If your current group of friends isn't helping you to become a better man—or if you simply don't have enough good friends—let me encourage you in the strongest way to develop some new friendships. Find some men of competence and character who care deeply about their own families, and get to know them. You'll find them wherever you find committed fathers: Boy Scouts troop leaders, sports coaches, church groups, family groups, and almost certainly at your work (yes, I guarantee you that there are some committed dads at your place of work—you just need to meet them).

There's also a toll-free 800-number counseling service available at www.FellowshipOfFathers.com that we call "Granddads on Call." This is a service staffed by dedicated, successful fathers who are also trained counselors. They have come through the trials of raising their own children and are dedicated to helping other men who might need some advice and encouragement. This service, which is available only to members of www.FellowshipOf Fathers.com (like yourself), has a small per minute service fee to cover its costs. Do check it out if you feel you would like to talk with an experienced dad on a specific fatherhood issue, or just in general. It never hurts to ask for some help.

The Benefits of Having Close Friends

True friends are not easy to find, especially in this day and age. And true friendships usually aren't built quickly; it normally takes time for a real friendship to develop. But a few real friends in your life can make all the difference. You need the friendship of at least one or two other men you can deeply trust, because these friends can (and will) help you in at least three critical ways:

1. *True friends will help you press on when the going gets tough.* Like a fellow Marine on a tough mission, a true friend will not let you abandon your post. If necessary, he will stand guard with you (as Pete did for Jon) in your darkest hours, and he will be there to celebrate with you when the new day breaks.

A Friend in Need

Jon was going through a very tough time with his wife. Three kids in six years, financial pressures and constant nagging from the in-laws had resulted in lots of tension at home and little physical intimacy with his wife. He had recently been asked by an old girlfriend to get together for drinks . . . and he was thinking that sounded pretty good. Sure, Jon loved his wife, but wasn't it okay to see an old friend?

When Jon mentioned this to his close buddy Pete, his friend had the courage (and the commitment to being a real friend) to ask a few honest questions. As Jon answered Pete's questions, he began to see why it might not be such a good idea to see his old girlfriend, especially at night in a bar for drinks. With Pete's encouragement, Jon cancelled the "date." Instead, he invited his wife out for a romantic dinner and gave her roses at the restaurant. Suffice it to say that physical intimacy was not a problem that evening . . . and with help, their marriage slowly healed. Now, almost 12 years later, Jon's marriage has never been better.

It's hard to know what would have happened had Pete not had the courage and the commitment to ask Jon some tough questions, but even Jon admits it might have been a total disaster.

2. *True friends will remind you of what is really important.* We live in a world where it is easy to forget what is true and what is important. Good friends—men who know you and know your family—won't let you forget those things, especially when the temptation of immediate gratification comes calling.

3. *True friends will point you to the Ultimate Source.* My best friends don't all believe exactly what I have come to believe, but all of them—to a man—believe in God. They

help remind me that no matter how tough things might be, I have a heavenly Father who loves me, who is committed to me, and who will see me through.

Of course, there are many other great benefits of having good friends. Research has repeatedly shown that men (and women) who have a close circle of friends live longer, stay healthier and enjoy happier lives on average than those who do not. These studies have controls for things like income, education and other variables, so they really are looking at the benefits of friendship itself.[2] It is also clear that the quality of one's friendships matter just as much as the quantity of the friendships. Sometimes it's easier for us guys to stay at a surface level, but we really do need at least one or two deep friendships.

Again, please understand me here: I'm not saying that you have to replace all your old friends—not at all. But as the old saying goes, "Bad friends ruin good morals." If you're spending too much time with guys who aren't helping you to become a better man, you need to think about expanding your circle of friends. Likewise, if you don't have a true friend in whom you can confide, you need one. Find some men of competence (good at what they do), character (honest and trustworthy) and commitment (faithful to their families, their friends and their communities). Strength and courage can be reinforced and multiplied between men of strength and courage—the whole is bigger than the sum of its parts. That is the beauty of the fellowship-of-fathers idea, and it's the reason we created www.FellowhipOfFathers.com. May it be a blessing to you and to millions of other strong and courageous men as well.

For Further Reflection

1. Think of your closest friends and pick three words for each guy that best describes him—the first words that come to mind are usually pretty accurate. What does the list look like? Strong? Mixed? Pretty sketchy? Be honest with yourself.

2. Have you ever shared your deepest fears, worries or struggles with any of these men? If so, did they help you face them and master them . . . or not?

3. Deep down, do you think you need to develop some new friendships with men of competence, character and commitment? Why or why not? If so, how do you plan to make that happen?

Today's Quick Wins

1. Take 60 seconds to think back to the best friend you've ever had and the best time you ever had together. Remember the laughter, the fun together and the good feelings that flowed from that friendship.

2. Take a few minutes today to drop a note or email an old friend you respect but with whom you've fallen out of touch. Spend some time catching up with him. Find out how he is doing and if you can help in any way. Do what you can to revitalize that friendship.

3. Take a few minutes to go to www.facebook.com/BeaBetterDad Today to see if there are other guys in your area who are reading this book and might want to get together with you. Or check out the many tools and services highlighted at www.Fel lowshipOfFathers.com to find opportunities to meet men of character, commitment and competence in your local area. Who knows, maybe you will make a new friendship or two.

Notes

1. *American Sociological Review*, as quoted in *USA Today*, June 22, 2006.
2. Lynne C. Giles, Gary F. V. Glonek, Mary A. Luszcz and Gary R. Andrews, "The Australia Longitudinal Study of Aging," *Community Health*, no. 59, 2005.

Developing High Quality Friendships with Other High Quality Men

I hope you agree with me that you need faithful friends if you are going to become the best dad you can be. So let's start with an honest assessment of the state of your friendships today. Ask yourself these three questions:

1. *How many true friends do you have in your life?* These are guys with whom you can share your fears, your feelings and your failings without fear of rejection or ridicule . . . and who can do the same with you. Of course, these will be friends you can have fun with, but the friendship needs to go deeper than just superficial sports talk or sharing a few laughs after work.

2. *How many friends do you have who are really good role models?* These are guys who fit into the first category but extend beyond it. These are men who love their families and who have had some success as a husband and father. In short, these are guys you respect for the job they are doing as a husband and father—guys you can learn from and learn with on the journey of life.

3. *How many of these friends can you count on to help you get back on the right path when you've gone astray?* These are guys who probably fit into groups #1 and/or #2, but

who are also among your closest friends. These are men who are close enough to you that they can ask you the really tough questions of life and hold you accountable to the higher standards you both share. These are men who won't just accept your reasons and excuses for behavior that you both know is not right. They will lovingly hold you to a higher standard, help you admit your failings, find forgiveness and get moving forward again. This is the type of friend the Bible talks about when it says, "There is a friend who sticks closer than a brother" (Proverbs 18:24, *NIV*). You are truly blessed if you have even just one friend like this.

Hopefully, you have at least a few buddies like these. But then again, if you're like 25 percent of American men, you don't have any close friends at all. That is like being in a foxhole all by yourself with the enemy advancing toward you—you are in trouble. Just like the Marine in the foxhole, you need at least a couple of buddies to support you, encourage you and help you get up again when you've been wounded.

Maybe you have some close buddies who fit into the first category, but they aren't exactly role models—or even close. While I would never encourage anyone to drop an old friend, the reality is that we all need friends who can help us learn and grow. We need other men who will challenge us and help us to be the best men we can be . . . and not just friends who can help us play and/or party.

So, how do you develop close, enduring, positive friendships with other men of character, commitment and quality? It takes three things:

1. *Frequenting the places where you are most likely to find men of this caliber.* If you are accustomed to frequenting places where guys are getting drunk and chasing women, it's pretty clear you're not going to be finding any positive and productive male role models. You might think it's hard to find other men like this, but in fact it's quite

easy, if you look for them in the right places. Who are the guys coaching your son's sports teams? Who are your kids' Cub Scout or Girl Scout leaders? Who are the dads who show up at your child's school play or band concert? Who are the dads running the fathers' programs at your local church? Join a men's Bible study—your pastor, priest, or chaplain can help you find one. If everything else fails, or if you just want a kick-start, you can go to www.FellowshipOfFathers.com and connect with the Facebook page to help you locate other dedicated dads who are interested in deeper, high quality friendships.

2. *A natural connection and a willingness to be open.* Let's face it: You won't hit it off with everyone. No one does. That is fine—in fact, that is probably a good thing. But you need to be open to deeper friendships with men with whom you share a lot in common (point #1) and with whom you just naturally connect. Some guys never let down their guard, and therefore never let a true friendship develop. Don't be one of those guys. Be open to new friendships with other major league dads. Who knows? The guy you met at your son's Boy Scouts meeting last night might be a true all-star dad who recently moved into the neighborhood and would really enjoy getting the two families together.

3. *Time and commitment.* There's no getting around it: Real friendships take time and a commitment to develop. No matter how many major league dads you might know—and no matter how many of these guys you feel a natural affinity for—you are never going to develop a real friendship if you are not willing to spend time with that person. Likewise, there has to be a commitment on both sides to deepen the friendship. That doesn't always happen—and that is fine. But when a

true mutual friendship *is* possible, both sides have to make time in order for it to happen.

Friendship with other good dads has been a key ingredient for every successful father I have ever known. I don't think you are going to be different. We each need some close friends who are willing, ready and able to help us become the men we were always meant to be. But true friendship goes even beyond that noble goal, for friendship is one of the great blessings of life in and of itself.

We all need friends—every one of us. So let's be sure that at least some of our closest friends are other good dads who can help us, encourage us and teach us—and for whom we can be similarly helpful. Remember: There is no way we will become the best dads, husbands and men we can be without the help of some close friends. And having a few close friends in life makes the journey all the sweeter.

TOOL #9

Optimistic, Never-Surrender Attitude

No matter how tough things get, you can never, ever, quit on your family. Winning dads never quit, and dads who quit never win.

Be strong and courageous, because you will lead these people [your family] to inherit the land.
JOSHUA 1:6, *NIV*

Never give in. Never give in. Never, never, never, never . . . never give in.
SIR WINSTON CHURCHILL

If you would like to discuss any of this material via email, feel free to contact me at **gws@beabetterdadtoday.com**

Do you remember reading about Hernando Cortes, the feerless global explorer who took Mexico for Spain in 1521? I'm not a big fan of Cortes, except for one thing he did. When he arrived in Mexico, he was one of the first Europeans to ever see that great land. He had a tiny group of soldiers and sailors with him. He was up against tens of thousands of Aztec warriors, a legendary Aztec chief and a great Aztec civilization that spread over thousands of miles. His men were scared, and many wanted to turn back. Cortes faced a mutiny among his already small force. So what did he do?

He burned his ships. By doing so, he eliminated his only means of escape and "bet it all" on his mission. He did not leave a path for quitting. It was victory . . . or death. Please don't misunderstand me. I'm not a fan of Cortes, and I don't agree with his methods, but there is a powerful lesson to be learned in the leadership decision he made. That lesson underscores the power of Tool #9: an Optimistic, Never-Surrender Attitude. By burning his boats, Cortes unified his team, put the past behind him, and went on to victory against overwhelming odds.

In our lives as husbands and fathers, there will be plenty of times when we will feel like throwing in the towel. There will be periods of conflict and discouragement with our wives. There will be episodes of intense disappointment and frustration with our kids. There will be times of fatigue, disillusionment and self-doubt in our lives. No dad, not one, escapes these challenges.

The question is not how to avoid these challenges—because the only way to do that is to *not* be a dad—but how to hang on through these difficult periods. Indeed, the real issue is how to learn from these challenges and grow through them so that we come out victorious on the other end. Again, that is why tool #8 is so important—we need other committed dads around us to bolster us in our times of weakness and encourage us in our times of need. It's also why we need to develop this tool: an Optimistic, Never-Surrender Attitude, and bring it out whenever needed.

Can't Have One Without the Other

I link the terms "optimistic" and "never surrender" because they are like two wheels on a bicycle. If you try to ride a bicycle with only one wheel, it will only be a matter of time before you fall over. Optimism without a never-surrender attitude is not sufficient to make a good marriage and a strong family stay upright. You really need them both.

A stoic, no-divorce-under-any-circumstances attitude is, in my opinion, a very good thing. It is a key portion of the superstructure of all strong marriages. But by itself it can also lead a husband and wife to a place of loneliness and even isolation, because one or both may believe that things will never get any better. That's where an optimistic attitude comes in. An optimist believes that no matter how bad things are, they can (and will) get better. Each of us is called to have this type of optimism in our marriages and family relationships.

If you have been married for more than a few months, you know that marriage has its ups and downs. This is true of every marriage, though some have more distinct (and difficult) swings than others. Sometimes things may get so tough that you and your wife might start to wonder why you ever got married in the first place. It is in times such as these that you must use your Optimistic, Never-Surrender Tool.

Maybe you think that sounds phony or ridiculous, but I assure you it is not. As a husband and father, you are the leader of the family. Whether you want to be or not doesn't matter—you are the leader of your family, and you must act like it. In this case, that means being the one to remember the good things about your wife and the wonderful things about your family—especially when times get tough. It means remembering your Noble Family Vision and the beautiful picture it paints for your future together. It means remembering God's promises for a better tomorrow if you hang on through today. In the words of my teenagers, it means "manning up."

We don't much need our Optimistic, Never-Surrender Tool when the proverbial sun is shining and everyone in our family is doing great. We need it when things are rough and the outcome of the battle is very much in doubt.

Lessons from History

Remember the Battle of the Bulge, the final Nazi push to turn the tide at the end of World War II? General Anthony McAuliffe was the commander of U.S. forces at the all-important town of Bastogne, which was right in the center of the German offensive. When his forces were surrounded, almost out of ammunition and quite possibly about to be annihilated, the opposing German generals sent a detachment under the white flag to ask for the American's surrender. McAuliffe's response was the essence of the Optimistic, Never-Surrender Attitude: "NUTS!" Of course, the Germans didn't understand his response, but they understood he wasn't giving up. His troops, however, immediately understood that their leader believed in them and was optimistic about the eventual outcome.

You know the result. Bastogne never fell to the Nazis, in large part because of McAuliffe's response. The Battle of the Bulge turned into an overwhelming defeat for Hitler. In fact, that devastating defeat sealed the fate of the Third Reich.

Why am I citing a battle that occurred more than 65 years ago as an example of the power of the Optimistic, Never-Surrender Attitude? Because just as in General McAuliffe's situation, the enemy will sometimes come to you and ask for your surrender—though usually not under a white flag. He might come in the form of a bottle or a pill. He might come in the form of a tight skirt and a suggestive invitation. He might come in the form of a "friend" who tells you it's okay to give up on your wife because "you deserve it" or "she doesn't deserve you" or some other nonsense. This is when you need to put this tool into effect. Don't surrender; for once you do, there is no turning back.

Think about Sir Winston Churchill, one of the greatest heroes of Western civilization in the twentieth century. At the height of the Battle of Britain, when it looked like the Nazis might defeat the

Royal Air Force and go on to invade Britain unimpeded, Churchill stood firm. For years, many of his political opponents had talked down the threat posed by Hitler. In fact, some had even tried to appease Hitler's aggression by giving the Nazi leader what he wanted. Now some of them were even talking about suing for peace with Germany, which would have left Britain a defeated and broken nation.

Churchill would have none of it. He knew that surrendering to Hitler would mean even more death and destruction for his people than fighting it out. He also knew that once England surrendered, there would be no going back. So he urged his people to fight on, which they did. He did not lose his optimistic, never-surrender attitude . . . and as a result, he never lost. He helped England stand against the Nazis, and by doing so he turned the tide of the war. At the end of his life, he was respected and revered by one and all on both sides of the Atlantic. My friend, we can learn a lot about life from Sir Winston Churchill.

Never Give In

If you are married but contemplating divorce or separation, unless it's for reasons of infidelity or physical violence, don't do it. I understand that you might be feeling terrible and that things might be very tough. I've been there. Most dads have. But the statistics are clear: The large majority of men who get divorced end up wishing they had not, and second marriages are almost twice as likely to fail as first marriages. In addition, as we've already discussed, children whose parents get divorced are almost twice as likely to get divorced themselves as those who grew up in two-parent households, not to mention that they are almost twice as likely to fall into drugs or alcohol abuse, end up in jail and have children out of wedlock.

You might have heard somewhere that a good divorce is better for the kids than an unhappy marriage. I think that line was invented by the American Divorce Lawyers Association, because it has no basis in reality. Research data is clear on this important

Winning Dads Never Quit; Quitting Dads Never Win

A friend of mine named Dan (not his real name) was married to an unusually lovely woman whose only real fault was that she had a truly terrible temper. When she felt ill or when it was that time of the month, she could erupt like a volcano. She would dredge up stuff from years back and berate Dan to no end, and then a few hours later, she would apologize and ask him to forgive her. She was never physically violent, and she generally didn't erupt when the children were around. Overall, Dan felt they had a pretty good marriage, but his wife's extreme temper sometimes led him to the brink of despair.

My friend had a choice—as we all do. He could have left his wife and kids . . . and that was an option he briefly considered. But as he thought about it, he realized that divorce was not the answer, as it would have left the kids dramatically worse off. Dan was aware of the overwhelmingly negative data about children of divorced parents, and he could see that might well be the case for his kids. He knew that his wife would probably be worse off, as she had come from a highly dysfunctional family as a child where anger and emotional abandonment were used as weapons. His leaving her would only make those childhood issues worse. He was also wise enough to realize that a divorce would leave him a weaker, poorer and probably lonelier man overall.

So Dan hung in there. He and his wife went for counseling, and they worked hard on their communication skills. Dan sharpened his Heartfelt Love Tool and learned to have it ready at all times. Little by little, over the months and years, his wife's severe anger problem got better. I wish I could tell you it disappeared entirely, but life is not a fairy tale. Maybe it will someday, maybe it won't. That's not the point.

Dan held on. He burned his boats (by deciding not to go for a separation or divorce). He strengthened his Optimistic, Never-Surrender Tool and became a stronger man, a better father and a more loving husband in the process. While things are not perfect at Dan's home today, he will be the first to tell you that they are much better than they were—and they are far better than what they probably would have become if Dan had taken the "easy way out." Dan is truly a major league dad—an All-Star in my book. My hat is off to him.

subject: Children of intact families, even families where there is significant emotional stress, are significantly more likely to graduate from high school (and college), stay out of jail, be emotionally stable and have a good family themselves than their peers whose parents chose to divorce.[1] Please note that I am not talking about physical or emotional abuse here. Those are completely unacceptable and need to be dealt with courageously to protect the victims. I am talking about the stresses and strains that are reality in most marriages and that, in some marriages, are an ongoing and serious challenge.

The truth is that divorce, which is so often portrayed as the easy way out, is the equivalent of an emotional abortion for the children involved. Sorry to be so graphic about it, but it's important to get the truth on the table.

So remember Cortes, McAuliffe and Churchill. Be courageous. Burn your boats and sharpen your Optimistic, Never-Surrender Tool. Sit down for a heart-to-heart with your pastor, chaplain, rabbi or priest. Call up one or more true friends who have themselves decided to never surrender, and ask for counsel and support. If all else fails and you really need to talk to someone, give us a call on our "Granddads on Call" service. We will do whatever we can to help.

One of the great privileges of being a dad is that, in the words of the old *Blues Brothers* movie, "It's not over until we say it's over." That's true for us as fathers because, as the leaders of our families, if we decide to give up, it's over. Maybe not right away, but in time. But if we have the courage to never surrender and decide to make it through the tough times, better times are ahead. That's not just optimism; that's reality. So take courage, and make sure your

Optimistic, Never-Surrender Tool is ready and waiting whenever you need it.

For Further Reflection

1. If you are still married, do you really believe that your marriage can get better? If you don't think it can get better, have you spoken with your pastor, priest, rabbi or another professional who might be able to help? If not, why not?

2. Do you have any "escape boats" that you need to burn?

3. What would you be willing to do if it were guaranteed to help your marriage?

Today's Quick Wins

1. Take 60 seconds to reflect on the best and hardest thing you have ever accomplished in your life. How did that make you feel?

2. Take 60 seconds to envision your family getting happier, healthier and stronger over the next 5, 10 or 20 years. How good does that look?

3. Take 60 seconds to meditate on the fact that you are the one who holds that vision in the palm of your hand. Of course, your family will have key roles, but stop and think about the fact that your family's future is in your hands.

Note

1. Alan Booth and Paul R. Amato, "Parental Pre-Divorce Relations and Offspring Post-Divorce Well-being," *Journal of Marriage and Family*, no. 63, February 2001.

Putting Your Optimistic, Never-Surrender Toolset to Work

The Optimistic, Never-Surrender Toolset has components that you might not need every day. Certainly you won't need them when the sun is shining, the kids are all getting along beautifully, and everyone thinks you're the greatest thing since sliced bread. But if you've been a father for more than a few months (actually, it's probably more like a few days), you know there are a whole lot of days when this isn't the case. It is at these times, where things are really tough, that you are most going to need the Optimistic, Never-Surrender Tool. So, how can you exercise this tool so you are sure it's ready for use when you need it the most?

First, you have to recognize the truth that life—for all of us—is *all* about the proper response. That is to say, in this life junk happens, and it happens all the time. You can't control it, you don't wish for it, and (hopefully) you try your best to avoid it. But it still happens. The only thing you can control is your response.

Someone will cut you off in traffic, and you will need to decide how to respond. Someone will diss you behind your back, and you will need to determine how you will react. Or someone in your family will have a bad day and get angry with you without cause, and you will need to figure out what you will say or do. In each of these situations, you can choose to strike back against those who are doing this to you (the improper response), or you can choose to take the higher road and choose to calmly ignore it or work it out with the person (the proper response). The power to make that decision is completely under your control.

Second, you have to realize that life's bigger challenges come for a reason. I know, I know—we all wish they didn't come at all. When a loved one falls seriously ill, or a family member loses a job, or a partner tries to cheat us on a business deal . . . these can be life-changing challenges. In fact, believe it or not, they were *meant* to be life-changing challenges. In truth, none of us is born with a well-developed Optimistic, Never-Surrender Attitude. In fact, all of us are born with no such skills to speak of. Fortunately, God does not want us to remain emotional infants, which is one of the reasons He allows big challenges into our lives.

As James wrote, "Count it all joy, my brethren, when you encounter various trials" (James 1:2, *NASB*). The apostle Paul certainly knew this secret. He faced huge challenges, bigger than any we are likely to ever face—wrongful imprisonment, vicious persecution and ongoing physical infirmity, to name just a few (see 2 Corinthians 11:25-28). But in overcoming these challenges, Paul built up his own Optimistic, Never-Surrender Toolset. He became a true overcomer, and his response was the right one no matter what or who tried to provoke him. At the end of his life, he was wrongfully sentenced to death. He probably could have recanted his faith and lived, but he realized that would be going back on all he had lived for. So he drew on his never-surrender attitude and went to his death—and in so doing literally changed the course of history. Paul had learned the source of inner strength in the face of life's toughest challenges, and he even shared it with us: "I know what it is to be in need, and I know what it is to have plenty. I have learned the secret of being content in any and every situation, whether well fed or hungry, whether living in plenty or in want. I can do everything through him who gives me strength" (Philippians 4:12-13, *NIV*).

That is the third realization: Our Optimistic, Never-Surrender Tool is powered by the certain knowledge that nothing happens without a reason. No matter how hard the trial or difficult the challenge, we are meant to overcome it and to learn and grow in the process. Remember: The hotter the fire, the stronger the steel. So give thanks when you face challenges big or small—and overcome them. Each time you do you will be strengthening this tool and growing into the father, the husband and the man you were always meant to be.

TOOL #10

Dynamic, Whole-Person Support

It is critically important for you to support your family emotionally, physically, mentally and spiritually—not just financially.

"Love the Lord your God with all your heart and with all your soul and with all your mind and with all your strength. . . . Love your neighbor as yourself." There is no commandment greater than these.
MARK 12:30-31, *NIV*

I always thought growing up that a father's job was just to "bring home the bacon." And while that is part of it, I now see that there's a lot more to it than just that.
JOE C., LONG ISLAND, NEW YORK

If you would like to discuss any of this material via email, feel free to contact me at **gws@beabetterdadtoday.com**

What does it mean for a father to support his family? When I heard that term, I used to think only of financial support. I would bet that most fathers have that same reaction, especially those of us who grew up in North America. But financial support, while important, is only one part of the critical support we need to provide for our families. In fact, I would argue that American culture puts too much importance on financial support while placing too little emphasis on emotional, physical, intellectual and spiritual support. The reality is that these four elements of the Dynamic, Whole-Person Support Tool are like the four tires on your car. If one is fully pumped up but the others are half inflated, your car isn't going anywhere fast.

Don't get me wrong; I'm not saying that fathers don't need to bring home the bacon. We sure do, sometimes by ourselves and sometimes with help from others. And sometimes, if things are tough on the job front, it might be up to others in our family (hopefully for only a short amount of time) to support our children financially. Being a financial supporter for the family is a critical support role that fathers must play. But it is only one of his roles. So let's take a look at the other four.

Emotional Support

What is emotional support? Why is it important? And how do you as a dad supply it anyway? Here's a secondary question I hear a lot from fellow dads: Isn't the emotional support for our kids supposed to come primarily from the mom? Aren't women naturally wired to be emotionally supportive?

To answer the first question, emotional support admittedly is a term that covers a lot of ground. But, in general, emotional support is being sure that each member of your family knows that you are with them and for them . . . always. Your emotional support will help your family members develop a deep-seated sense of quiet self-confidence, which is so vital to us as human beings.

If you are married, and if she knows that you are truly for her and for your family (before personal success, for example), over time she will grow more confident in your marriage and in your future together. Also, over time she will grow more confident in your ability to lead your family in the right direction. This is especially important when tough decisions have to be made to move your family through the storms and trials of life. In those difficult times when you and your family are facing tough decisions, it is critical that your life partner knows that you are with her and for her . . . period.

Providing effective emotional support for your wife is not always going to be easy. You must learn to be a student of your wife, understanding her moods, concerns, strengths and weaknesses. This is where the Relationship Tools we talked about in Tool #6 come in to play. You must learn how to listen to your wife so that you understand how to communicate *love* in a way that is meaningful to her. Like a beautiful and delicate snowflake, every woman is different. What would be effective emotional support for some women will be less effective with others.

At its core, your support for your wife will give her the confidence and conviction that you are committed to her, love and appreciate her, and will be there for her (and the kids) when the going gets tough. This will not only make her a more secure and confident human being, but it will also enable her to provide critical emotional support to your children. For when she is confident and content herself, she can better convey love and care to your children.

Just as with your wife, your children must also know in their heart of hearts that you treasure them and will always be there for them. Over time, if you as a dad wield the Dynamic, Whole-Person Support Tool wisely and consistently with your children, they will come to understand deep down that that they are valuable, important and worthy of respect. As a result, I sincerely believe that they will grow up to be more mature and more caring human beings. It is no accident that God's Word tells us that loving others starts in our own hearts. In fact, Jesus says the second most important commandment of all is to love others as you love yourself (see Mark 10:31). There are many different interpretations of that verse, but to me it means that to truly and sincerely care for

The Importance of Emotional Support

My friend Tim married a woman who had come from an extremely difficult childhood. Abandoned by her parents, she had grown up in and out of foster homes. Her emotional security levels were quite low and her emotional defense barriers were, understandably, very high. Sometimes she would retreat into a cone of silence for reasons Tim did not understand. But Tim didn't give up the ship. He observed his wife carefully and noticed that (like most wives) she deeply appreciated his being home in time for dinner. She also loved to get a quick phone call or two from him during the day. And she lit up like a little girl when he brought her small gifts or flowers.

Tim realized that these were things she had not been given as a child; regular family dinners, daily calls from loved ones, and little "I love you" gifts simply were not part of her childhood. None of this was expensive or difficult for Tim to do, but his doing them on a regular basis made all the difference to his wife. Over time, she opened up more and more to him. Their marriage flourished, and she became a wonderful mother to their three great kids. I won't say that things in their house are always perfect, because I don't want to lie. But because Tim learned to use the Dynamic, Whole-Person Support Tool effectively, she has overcome an extremely difficult childhood, and today they are a truly happy family.

others, a person must have a healthy and appropriate self-image. A dad's emotional commitment to his children helps develop those inner resources in his kids.

This doesn't mean that you coddle your two- or three-year-old when he or she throws a temper tantrum. Neither does it mean that you accept without comment all the behavior of your teenager. Quite the opposite, in fact. But if you've built up your children's emotional security over the years, and if you have disciplined them in the right way, your children will know deep down that you are doing this for their own good. They will know at their core that they are lovable and valuable, because they have been loved and valued by you.

The ways in which we demonstrate emotional support to family members is going to be different depending on their age, their gender and the situation. When your three-year-old girl is scared because of a thunderstorm, emotional support for her is a big hug and maybe a cup of hot chocolate (and, if it's a bad storm, maybe she snuggles up with you and Mom for the rest of the night). If your 23-year-old son just got a rejection slip from the company he really wanted to work for, emotional support for him would be to go out somewhere together and remind him what a good young man he is. You would probably tell him a couple stories about times when you were laid off or didn't get that "dream job"—and help him realize that it is not the end of the world. More importantly, you help him realize that you, as his dad, have real confidence in him. Sure, there are going to be disappointments along the way. Life is tough. But he will overcome those challenges, and you will be there cheering him on.

At every age, children need the emotional support of their mother and their father. That's what emotional support is all about. So use it frequently. Don't be afraid to let your kids know how much you love them and how proud you are of them. Let them know they are special—because they are. And be sure to let them know in both word *and* action.

Physical Support

Some dads, because of their upbringing or their nature, tend not to be physically affectionate with their children (or their wives). In my view, this is a real mistake. Research has proven over and over the huge benefits to babies and young children of appropriate physical affection (in fact, the gruesome Nazi experiments of World War II proved that babies without physical affection shrivel up and die—always—even if they were given everything else they needed).

The human need for physical support is a basic human need. Like water, we cannot live without it. So let's not withhold from our kids something they cannot live without. Of course, it always has to be given in an age- and context-appropriate way—but it has to be given. Men, we cannot let our own upbringing or fear of rejection, or whatever it is, hinder us from providing for our sons, our daughters and our other family members something they need and long for: our physical support.

If giving appropriate physical support is a problem for you, get some counseling and help with this. If your kids are not with you right now, resolve in your heart to make giving them a hug the very first thing you do when you see them next. Then work through the Put It to Work Guide at the end of this chapter to see how you can truly become a physically supportive dad in the best way possible.

Another element of physical support is making sure that your children eat well, sleep enough and get at least 60 minutes of physical exercise each day. No, I am not saying that you need to fix three healthy meals, tuck everyone in at night *and* play an hour of sports with each of your kids every day. But I am saying that as the leader of your household, you set the example in everything. If you're overweight, eat badly, smoke, drink to excess and/or watch too much TV . . . the odds are very strong that your kids are going to follow your example (no matter what you say).

So set a good personal example in this area (as well as in all the others) and do everything you can to help your children develop a healthy lifestyle. Be sure that your kids have healthy snacks around the house (get rid of the chips and soda). Be sure they are getting a minimum of eight hours of good sleep every night. And be sure that they are getting out with friends or at school to exercise properly. Those things are not hard to do if you and your children's mother agree they are important (and they are). This basic physical support will help your children develop better in all other areas (emotionally, academically, athletically and intellectually), and it will dramatically reduce their chances of suffering from the twenty-first-century plague that is impacting American kids by the millions: childhood obesity and early onset diabetes.

Physical Support Is a Basic Human Need

I remember a friend of mine named Michael (not his real name) who was raised by a strict and physically unsupportive father of Scandinavian heritage. It was a real struggle for Michael to give his young daughter any kind of physical affection, even a gentle hug or a pat on the back. Over the years, his daughter started to seek out physical support from other sources—primarily from somewhat older men. This was not a positive development in any way. When Michael and his wife sat down to confront their daughter about this, she had a lot of excuses. For a while she continued to justify behavior she knew in her heart was wrong. But after a while, she simply broke down and said to Michael, "Dad, I just need you to show me you love me."

Michael was cut to the core. He had always loved his daughter, but he realized that he had not shown her the physical and emotional support she desperately needed. He decided then and there that he could not continue the generational curse that had been handed down to him. And he resolved to do whatever he needed to do to win back his daughter. It was not an easy road, but over time, Michael and his daughter developed a much better father/daughter relationship—including some appropriate physical support (holding hands, a gentle kiss on the forehead, a nice hug from time to time). To this day, Michael credits the wake-up call he got at that meeting with his beloved daughter.

Childhood obesity and its stepsister, early onset diabetes, are at close to epidemic proportions among our youth. These are crippling diseases that doom most sufferers to lives of ongoing pain, dramatically reduced overall health and mobility, and (frequently) an early death. And these diseases are largely preventable. So let's do our part for our children and make sure they are not part of this terrible scourge.

> ## The Critical Importance of Reading to and with Our Children
>
> A dear friend recently sent me this note: "Over the years, we have been consistent in setting aside 10 minutes or so after dinner and before bedtime to read with our kids. This has included not only books but also magazines like *Sports Illustrated* and the day's news-paper. We have found reading to be a great way to learn to-gether—and to teach our sons the importance of mastering the skill of reading. In the same way, reading just a few minutes each day with your sons and/or daughters will help them develop a life-long love of reading and learning. That's one of the best gifts you can give your children, and there's no time like the present to begin to give them that gift. So start today . . . or the next time you see them. Bring a good book or a magazine they will enjoy. Even comic books are good—whatever they like to read and en-joy. That is a great gift that you can give to your kids as their dad.

Intellectual Support

Do you know that reading to your children when they are young is one of the best things you can do to ensure their academic and pro-fessional success later in life? That's right. Research is overwhelm-ingly clear on this point. Young children who have fathers and mothers who read to them regularly perform significantly better ac-ademically through all levels of schooling than their less-fortunate peers. They are much more likely to graduate from high school, college and even graduate school. They tend to earn significantly more at their jobs than those who did not grow up in intellectually nurturing homes. And their children tend to do better academically as well.[1]

What an encouraging note . . . and again, the research totally backs it up. So if you want your children to do well academically when they are older (as well as now), read to them every day when they are younger. Even 10 minutes a night is helpful.

Taking the time to answer your children's questions about nature, the universe, history or whatever will also help them build a cohesive understanding of our world. It will give them the confidence to ask questions, to explore and to push into areas they don't totally understand. If you can't be with your children on a daily basis, encourage your wife (or children's mother) or other caregivers to make reading to them a priority. When you see your children, make a point to ask them about what they are reading, and also ask if they have any questions or discoveries to share.

When we first took our children to Europe, I was amazed at how much our sons knew about the battles of World War II. They were able to tell us about Allied and Axis troop movements on D-Day—details that were far beyond my general understanding. Of course we had a great time, and it was no small point of pride for our boys that they were able to instruct their parents in the history of those great conflicts.

Each child is different; some will be more academically minded, while others will excel in different areas. This is normal—and good. We have tried to discover the natural strengths of each of our children and have deliberately tried to help each of them maximize those strengths. Every child does have natural strengths . . . and weaknesses. But every child also needs to have a baseline of academic abilities: reading, writing and mathematics at least at their grade level. In developing those skills over time, kids also learn organization, self-discipline and critical thinking skills. No matter what they decide to do as a profession, even if they work with their hands as a mechanic or bricklayer or zookeeper (all very honorable endeavors), our kids are going to need these basic intellectual skills. Without them, they will be relegated to unskilled manual labor jobs that pay minimum wage, no matter how "smart" they are intuitively.

Supporting our children's intellectual development is one of the most important jobs we have as fathers. Of course, we cannot do it by ourselves, nor should we try to do so. Their mothers, our older children, teachers, mentors and extended family members all play key roles in the intellectual development of our children. But we cannot outsource our responsibility in this critical area. It is up to us, along with our wives (or children's mother), to ensure that our children have the intellectual support they need and deserve.

Spiritual Support

The Bible is very clear about our responsibility to raise up our children spiritually as well as mentally and emotionally. "Train up a child in the way he should go; even when he is old he will not depart from it" is an often-quoted scriptural promise from the book of Proverbs (22:6, *ESV*). But the Bible has much more to say about the key roles that we as dads need to play in the spiritual (including the moral and ethical) development of our kids.

It is a fact that you are the spiritual leader of your homes. You cannot delegate that responsibility to Mom, the church, the schools or anyone else. Of course you need partners in this effort— and, if you are married, your primary spiritual partner needs to be your wife. Finding good men who will partner with you in this effort is also important, as we discussed in Tool #8, "Other Good Dads." But make no mistake: Your wife and your children will look to you for spiritual leadership. That is not going to change.

I'm afraid that too many dads today—even Christian dads— are not taking this important responsibility seriously. And if we don't take it seriously, who will?

Yes, I certainly agree that when our sons and daughters are fully grown, they can and must decide for themselves the right path to take spiritually, morally and ethically. But as their fathers, we have the God-given responsibility to teach them when they are young what is good and right and true and just, to the very best of our ability. If we don't do this, no one else will. This is a big part of what we discussed in Tool #3 on the importance of having a True Moral Compass.

Pop culture is all around us, as is the relentless advertising of Madison Avenue. Pop culture worships those who push the limits, reject authority and "do it my way." Madison Avenue is always trying to convince us that we can't be truly happy without products

Getting Involved in Your Child's Spiritual Development

Jack didn't see his boys very much. He and their mom had never married, and just after the birth of his second son, he had been sentenced to three years in jail.

While Jack was serving his sentence, he developed a close friendship with the prison chaplain, who was a good man and a good father. The chaplain encouraged Jack to start praying for his boys—and for their mom—on a daily basis. After some prodding, Jack did just that. Some time later, the chaplain encouraged Jack to let his boys and their mom know that he was praying for them every day, which Jack also did.

One day, Jack was surprised to get a letter back from one of his boys thanking him for his prayers and asking if they could come visit. Jack had done what he could to help his boys spiritually . . . even from jail. They appreciated his prayers, as did their mom.

X, Y and Z; that fulfilling our personal wants is the key to happiness. That is another not too subtle lie, but it's one we hear almost every day from modern media. And Madison Avenue's use of sexually implicit and explicit advertising to sell us (especially the young) more stuff that we don't need is legendary. If we don't help our children develop a True Moral Compass, popular culture and Madison Avenue will step in to do the job. Add to that the fact that there are so many seriously dysfunctional families today that our kids are sure to have classmates, teammates or neighborhood kids who have never been taught right from wrong.

Net-net: Either we help our children develop a complete spiritual, ethical and moral framework for life—the True Moral Compass we talked about in Tool #3—or other forces in our society will do it for us. Unfortunately, in most cases those other forces will be pushing our children in a very different direction than we would have them go.

We touched on the subject of helping our children grow spiritually in Tool #7, "Heaven's Help," but the big secret is this: We cannot help our children grow spiritually, morally and ethically if we ourselves are not growing in these areas. Jesus Himself makes this clear for us in the Gospel of John when He talked about the fact that we must remain vitally connected to Him (like a branch to a tree) if we are to bear "much fruit" (John 15:5). Certainly a warm and loving family—and children who grow up to be a blessing to you and to society at large—is "fruit that endures." So let's not shirk our own responsibility to grow spiritually and provide the spiritual support that our younger children (and even, at times, our older kids) so desperately need.

Please take a look at the Put It to Work Guide at the end of this chapter, as well as the other tools and services for dads that can be found at www.FellowshipOfFathers.com. Remember, you need to be equipped to provide the emotional, physical, intellectual and spiritual support your children (and all children) need.

Again, remember that while financial support is very important, by itself it is not enough. In fact, it is not even close to enough. If you want to be a major league dad, you must learn to use all four of the skills in the Dynamic, Whole-Person Support Tool: emotional support, physical support, spiritual support and financial support—and you must learn to use them well. Just like the four tires on your car, if one of these skills is underinflated and underused, it probably means serious problems down the road.

For Further Reflection

1. Do you agree that dads need to play more than just a financial support role in the family? Why or why not? How would you say you are doing in each of the four dynamic support areas (emotional, physical, intellectual and spiritual) with your family?

2. Among the four areas, where are your biggest strengths? What are your biggest opportunities for improvement?

3. Do you have the courage to ask others for input on these questions? (I hope you do. Go for it.)

Today's Quick Wins

1. Take 60 seconds to think back to your own childhood. Remember some times when your mom or dad (or grandma or granddad) gave you the emotional or physical or intellectual or spiritual support that you needed. What did that mean to your wellbeing?

2. Take as much time as you need to pray deeply and sincerely for each of your children—and ask God to show you in your heart what type of support each one most needs from you right now. He will.

3. Take a few minutes to come up with an idea of how you might better provide that type of support, starting today. Then go do it, brother. There is nothing more important in this life.

Note

1. "Children Better Prepared for School If Their Parents Read Aloud to Them," *British Medical Journal*, May 2008.

Putting Your Dynamic, Whole-Person Support Toolset to Work

When it comes to providing emotional support, physical support, intellectual support and spiritual support for your family members, how are you doing? The truth is that it's not always easy to know, and the longer your family has gone without adequate support from you in one or more areas, the less they will expect. But one thing is for sure: No matter where you are with your Dynamic, Whole-Person Support Tool, you can get better. So here's an exercise to help you sharpen this tool starting today. For each member of your family, think and pray about where that individual needs the most support.

- Does your son need help with his homework?
- Does your daughter need to talk with you about her social life?
- Do others in your family need your help and encouragement on the spiritual front?

You probably have a sharper intuition than you think on these things. If you're really stumped for your kids, it's always a good idea to ask your wife or children's mother (they almost always have a very good sense of where their children are ... and where they might need the most help). Likewise, if you're struggling to determine how best to support her—you might ask your eldest daughter for her insights (especially if she is old enough to really understand your wife—say 18 and over). Once you have done this, follow these steps to put your Dynamic, Whole-Person Support Tool to work:

1. Take a piece of paper and make three columns on it.

2. In the left-hand column, write the name of each member of your family.

3. In the middle column, list the type of support you believe that family member needs the most (emotional, physical, intellectual or spiritual).

4. In the right-hand column, list the ways that you could provide that support (helping your son with homework, praying with your family, spending time with your daughter to help her with a specific problem she is having, and so on).

5. Put your plan into practice over the next 30 days and see what happens. I guarantee your family will be blessed as long as you follow through with your plan. Not only that, but you will have sharpened your Dynamic, Whole-Person Support Tool considerably.

If you're happy with the results, why not repeat the exercise the next month? Switch up the type of support you are providing each family member (unless someone really needs concentrated support in one area). Practice using various support tools, and you will grow more skilled with each. And did I mention how blessed your family will be?

If you're not happy with the results after 30 days, be sure to ask yourself three questions:

1. *Did I really execute my 30-day dynamic support plan for my family?* Did you stick to it and get it done as planned?

Or did you kind of drop the ball halfway through? Be honest with yourself . . . a lack of follow-through might be the problem.

2. *Was I focused on the areas of dynamic support that each family member needed, or was I off target a bit?* In executing your 30-day dynamic support plan, you might have discovered that one or more family members have even bigger needs. If that's the case, you probably want to refocus your efforts. It's always important to focus on the biggest issues.

3. *Is there a bigger issue that I need help to address?* If you truly executed your 30-day dynamic support plan and were focused on the right areas for each family member but it still didn't work, it's probably time to talk. Sit down individually with each member of your family and let them know what you were trying to do (trust me, they will be blessed just to hear that you were thinking of them and trying to help). Ask what worked well and what didn't work at all. Get on the same page—the discussion alone should be very helpful—and then put it to work in the next 30 days. It will be a good experience for you and each member of your family.

PART THREE

Special Situations

1

Being the Best Single Dad You Can Be

As a single dad, you are still irreplaceable in your children's lives—and always will be. Don't ever forget that . . . and don't let them forget you.

It's not the critic that counts, not the man who points out how the strong man stumbled or whether the doer of deeds could have done them better. . . . The credit belongs to the man who is actually in the arena, whose face is marred by dust, and sweat and blood, who strives valiantly, who errs and frequently comes up short again and again. Who knows the great enthusiasms, the great devotions and spends himself in a worthy cause.

PRESIDENT THEODORE ROOSEVELT

When I got divorced, I pretty much gave up on ever being a real father to my kids. But now I see that was totally wrong. They still need me. In some ways they need me even more now. And I want to be there for them.

SCOTT P., SAVANNAH, GEORGIA

If you would like to discuss any of this material via email, feel free to contact me at **gws@beabetterdadtoday.com**

Real life is not easy for anyone, and sometimes we make it even harder for ourselves. As the old saying goes, "Life is what happens when you're making other plans." So maybe you find yourself trying to raise your kids as a single dad. Or maybe you have joint custody with your ex-wife. Or maybe you don't even see your kids much these days. Or maybe you (or your ex-wife) are part of a new "blended" family. Each of these situations is different, and each one has its own set of complications and challenges. I don't want to minimize how difficult some of those might be, but here's the good news: No matter what the situation, your kids still need you—and you are still their dad.

Let me also take a moment to say "thank you," because if you are still reading this book, you love your children, and that means a great deal.

Sure, there will be critics. I've noticed in my life that there is usually no lack of people to tell me how they would have done it better when I come up short. But as Teddy Roosevelt reminds us on the previous page, the true credit belongs to the man who is actually in the arena, slugging it out for his family and his children, no matter what. I appreciate that you care so deeply about your kids, especially as a single dad. Again, thank you.

So in this chapter, let's look at a few different situations in which a single dad might find himself. Feel free to skip right to the section that is of most interest to you. And remember, there's a lot more info, help and encouragement on each of these at wwwFellowshipOfFathers.com, which I hope you will check out. But for now, let's look at how a single dad can use his fatherhood toolset to be the best dad he can be.

For Fathers Separated from Their Kids

My friend, if you find yourself in this difficult situation, the words of Sir Winston Churchill are for you: "Never, never, never give up." I know that for a dad who is separated from his children, one of the easiest things to do is to just give up trying to get closer. Please don't do it.

Just as the fate of the British Empire hung on the decision of Prime Minister Churchill not to give up, the future of your children hangs, in large part, on the decision you make about them. You and I both know in our hearts that our kids need us. They need us in different ways as they progress through childhood into adolescence and beyond. But they need us even as they pass into adulthood and become parents themselves. We've talked about it earlier: The statistics could not be clearer or more powerful. So don't give up on your kids—no matter how bad things might look right now or how long it's been since you saw them last.

Of course, every situation is different, and if you've been separated from your children for many years, it will be hard to reconnect with them. But I can tell you one thing for sure: No matter how difficult it might be, it is far, far better than dying alone, separated from them emotionally and spiritually.

You might be saying to yourself, *How do you know that, Gregory?* Good question. I know this from personal experience. As I mentioned at the start of this book, my dad decided to separate himself from our family . . . entirely. For many years no one heard from him, despite our repeated attempts to contact him. He had decided to live for himself, and he ended up literally dying by himself. He was alone, in semi-squalor and what was clearly deep loneliness, depression and sadness.

So if you are in that difficult situation and are truly separated from your kids, make up your mind right now to bridge the gap, dismantle the walls, and get back in the game as their dad. You probably will want to start with a letter or email (it's usually best not to just show up unannounced) explaining your change of heart and apologizing—yes, *apologizing*—for whatever you might need to ask forgiveness for. Trust me, I know that apologizing sounds like a tough thing to do . . . and sometimes it is. But it is also freeing, and it can help your children turn the page on what might be a difficult past. No matter how you do it, decide today to get back in your kids' lives as a positive force for good.

Do it step by step. Remember that Rome wasn't built or rebuilt in a day. A heartfelt letter or email, with an apology if necessary, is a

Love Never Fails

A man I know named Stephen left his wife high and dry for another woman and then initiated divorce proceedings. His wife, a lovely lady, was devastated, as were their children. Stephen, never one to care much about others' feelings, didn't pay them much heed. Things between him and his ex-wife grew progressively worse until communication virtually ceased. Of course, their children (rightly) held their dad responsible for the breakup of their family . . . and held that anger deep inside. Mom began to battle deep depression, and the kids began to indulge in self-destructive behavior. The situation was heading toward disaster.

Then one day, a good friend invited Stephen to a great church in his city. Stephen didn't want to go, but he did. That day the pastor happened to preach a sermon on God the Father's love for earthly fathers (do you think that was a coincidence?). Stephen's stony heart was pierced by the kindness and truth of God's Word to him that day. He went forward to confess and forsake his sin and to ask God's help going forward.

Stephen then went home and wrote a letter of apology to his ex-wife and each of his kids. The letters were sincere and heartfelt, and they began a sea change in the life of that former family. Over time, his ex-wife had the grace to forgive Stephen, reversing the tide of bitterness that had been rising in her heart. Stephen and his children reconciled, and he once again became their dad. Stephen and his ex-wife have not remarried—so we will keep praying for that—but each family member is on a much better path, and the family as a whole is healing and moving forward. In place of almost certain disaster, they are now headed (most of the time) toward a stronger and better future, and all because of Stephen's change of heart. God's love didn't fail Stephen . . . so his love didn't fail his family.

good place to start. Maybe suggest a phone call as a next step—gently. If the offer isn't immediately accepted, don't be hurt. Wounds, especially the deepest ones, take time to heal. Write or email again a few weeks later (be sure you have a correct address) and simply speak from your heart about your desire to rebuild your relationship and be the best dad you can be.

Trust me: Those emails or letters will be a balm to the wounds of your son or daughter (or ex-wife), no matter what their age or situation. They will be good for your soul as well. Eventually, if you keep on, you will get a response. It might be hesitant at first, or it might even be negative. Don't worry about that—at least you're back in touch with your son or daughter. That alone is something over which you can rejoice. It's also something on which you can build. You might have to apologize again, which is okay. Be honest about it: If you have really hurt your kids—or allowed them to be hurt—they deserve the right to tell you about that hurt and to have you ask for their forgiveness . . . multiple times. That is part of the healing process—a very big part, in fact.

Step by step, first in writing, and then over the phone, and then, finally, face to face when circumstances and emotions permit, you can work to rebuild those key relationships. Sure, you might have to ask your ex-wife's permission, and she might say no. Face it, my friend: If you've been separated from your kids for years, it's going to take time to rebuild those relationships, and that goes double for your wife or ex-wife. Badly damaged relationships—like people—take time and tender, loving care to heal. But heal they can, and heal they must if you, and they, are to be all God intended you both to be.

Remember that your son or daughter will always be your son or daughter . . . and they will always need you. Take the first step today, maybe with the help of your pastor, chaplain, priest, rabbi or close friend. And then don't stop. Rebuilding a real relationship with your kids will mean the world to them (trust me, I know what it would have meant to me), and it will also help you in a very big way.

For Widowers

If you are a widower, first and foremost, you have my deepest sympathies. There is nothing I can say that is worthy of your loss. But I will commend two words to your attention: "strength" and "courage." These are great and necessary assets for any dad, but they are especially important for dads who have lost their beloved wives much earlier in life than expected. Trying to raise good kids is hard enough with their mother at your side. On your own, you need special help. Maybe that's why throughout the Bible, we see that the Lord has a special place in His heart for the widow and the widower. So if you are a widower, know that God Almighty has a special concern for your welfare and that of your children. He knows the sorrow and the loss (His only Son died too). And He promises you His strength and courage for the new challenges that now lie before your family (see Joshua 1).

But there is another word I would like to bring to your attention, a word that we don't use much as men or dads: "accommodation." What do I mean by that? I mean that you almost certainly have to make changes as a result of losing your wife, the mother of your children, such as by taking a less demanding job or spending less time on your personal hobby or with your buddies. These types of accommodations will enable you to spend extra time with your kids, to just listen to them and be with them in their sadness and grief.

For Fathers Divorced from Their Wives

If you're separated or divorced from the mother of your kids, I'm going to give you some advice that you probably don't want to hear: *Be good to her.* I don't care what she did or didn't do. It doesn't matter. I don't mean that literally, because of course what we do and how we conduct ourselves matters. Actions have consequences—sometimes very negative ones. But what I am saying is this: What *really* matters most is that she is the mother of your children, and their future depends on her even more than it depends on you. So be nice to her in every way you possibly can.

Growing Closer in the Wake of Tragedy

One of our son's good friends—a really wonderful young man I will call Andrew—lost his mom in high school. After her death, I noticed how his dad made some changes in his work schedule to be home more often. He made other changes, too, changes that allowed him to be there more with his kids. While nothing could ever take away the pain of losing his mom, Andrew and his dad have grown even closer in the wake of the tragedy. That has happened because Andrew's dad knew his son would need him even more without the presence of his mom, so he made accommodation for that. Today, Andrew is one of the most mature and pulled-together young men I know . . . and his dad can take credit for that.

What's that you say? Impossible? Unrealistic? Naïve? No worries, my friend, I've been called much worse. But I am not going to give up on this point: You need to be respectful and kind to your ex-wife—always. I don't care if she (and your kids) is part of a new "blended" family, or if you are. You need to treat her with the respect she deserves as the mother of your children. Period.

I will admit that in many cases that will not be easy. In fact, there's only one way I know how to do that, especially if a great deal of bitterness and resentment has built up: *You must forgive her.* Yes, you heard me right. Even if she was the one to break her marriage vows—and the marriage—you must forgive her. Before you decide I am nuts on this, hear me out. There are three reasons you need to forgive your wife, and only one of them is directly related to her.

1. Forgive Her for Your Sake

First, *you need to do it for your own soul.* Do you think it was an accident that Jesus taught us in the Lord's Prayer, "Forgive us our debts as we also have forgiven our debtors" (Matthew 6:12, *NIV*)? That was no mistake. God knows the power of forgiveness. He knows that there cannot be love or peace or joy without forgiveness. The very fact that He has forgiven your sins gives you the power to forgive your ex-wife. For the Lord knew that old secret: Harboring bitterness is like drinking poison and waiting for the other person to die. It will kill you.

Think I'm exaggerating on that point? I am not. We all know men (and women) who have let bitterness slowly but surely disfigure and destroy their very soul. A guy I knew, whom I will call Bob, harbored such an intense hatred for his ex-wife that over time it literally made him ill (at least, the doctors felt it contributed to a very serious stomach ailment he developed). Eventually, Bob became an extremely bitter person who, frankly, was very difficult to be around. He blamed his ex-wife for everything, even things she had absolutely nothing to do with. Over time, his mental state became more and more separated from reality.

Finally, by God's grace, and through the faithful prayers of a few long-time friends and relatives (including his children) and their direct intervention, Bob came to realize that he had to let go of his bitterness. He realized that, just like a cancer, his anger was consuming him, and that the only way to defeat it was to forgive his ex-wife. I won't tell you that Bob was immediately healed in every respect. Life is not a fairy tale. But I do know that Bob sensed a deep peace inside him when he finally found the courage to forgive his ex-wife from his heart. I also know that his stomach condition is dramatically better—and he is a lot easier to be around these days. Forgiving his ex-wife was the best thing Bob could have done for himself. That is the first reason to forgive—it frees your own soul.

2. Forgive Her for Your Kids' Sake

Second, *you need to forgive your wife for your kids' sake.* Once you have truly forgiven your ex-wife, with God's help, you will be able to treat her more civilly and respectfully. As you behave well toward her, she will notice, and so will your kids. Yes, you will have to bite your tongue if ever (or whenever) she says something mean or nasty to you. You will have to be a man, take it and respond in kindness, which is something only truly strong men can do. Jesus' instruction to "bless those who curse you" (Luke 6:28, *NIV*) is difficult to do anytime, but especially when the curses are flowing from a family member who knows your hot buttons and deepest insecurities. But if you ask the Lord to help you to "overcome evil with good" (Romans 12:21, *NIV*), as He commands, He will do it. Your kids will notice—and they will be much better for it.

3. Forgive for Her Sake

Third, *you need to do it for her sake.* Here is another tough truth, brother: Very few divorces are truly the fault of only one party. In fact, statistics tell us that although more women file for divorce than men, it is usually in response to something the husband did, such as physical abuse, adultery, alcoholism or long-term joblessness. Studies on the subject tell us that the root cause of the majority of divorces starts with the husband.[1]

All I am saying here is that if you are honest with yourself, you will almost certainly have to admit that you also made serious mistakes in your former marriage. You will also have to admit, if you are honest with yourself, that there were actually good points about your ex-wife. And again, no matter what, you have to remember that she is and will always be the mother of your children. So do the right thing. Be a man. Forgive your ex-wife from your heart. You will be the better man for it—and it will be a true blessing to your kids and your ex-wife as well.

Of course, you can't just stop there. Obviously, you need to pay her whatever she is owed for child support, alimony, and so on. I know this may be unpopular in some circles, but there it is. You are still responsible for her and for your children, both legally and morally. Not only is it the law of the land, but it is also the right thing to do.

Just as important, you must treat your ex-wife with courtesy and respect and back her up when you are with the kids. How do you expect your sons to grow up to respect their wives if you do not model that behavior? How do you expect your daughters to marry good men who love and respect them if they don't see that in their own father? "Do as I say, not as I do" is a recipe for disastrous fatherhood. Guys, I know this isn't easy, but as dads, we need to set the example. If you want to be the best single dad you can be, you have to treat your ex-wife with courtesy and back her up when you are with the kids.

Take the Lead in Making Peace

One last thing on this subject: If you need to ask your wife or ex-wife to forgive you for certain things you said or did or didn't do, please do so. I know that you might think she needs to be the one to be forgiven. Heck, you might even be right on that. But even though you are divorced, you are still the servant leader of your family, and you are the one who has to take the lead in making peace, as tough as that may be. Jesus taught us all that "blessed are the peacemakers, for they will be called sons of God" (Matthew 5:9, *NIV*). I trust that you want to be counted among God's sons, so sit down and write a kind and thoughtful email or letter to your ex-wife and ask for her forgiveness for whatever needs to be forgiven. You will be amazed at the peace it will bring to your heart, even if she never answers you. Because whether or not she responds, the Lord will bless you in other ways for taking His path of peace.

It bears repeating: If you want to be the best single dad you can be for your kids, you need to forgive your ex-wife, honor and respect her and ask for her forgiveness if need be. These are the vital steps toward being the best single dad you can be. Again, I'm not saying this will be easy, but I am saying that you, your kids and your ex-wife will be deeply and richly blessed if you take these steps. I promise it. This is, unfortunately, a choice that few men make these days, and they wind up much the worse for it. Don't be like these men and end up bitter and separated from your children.

If you are separated, divorced or never married the mother of your children, do the right thing by her. Support her emotionally, financially and spiritually. Pray for her and for your kids. Be sure to support her verbally in front of the children, especially when she isn't there. If you are earning money, pay her alimony and child support on time and do your part to help her whenever you can. I know it will probably take months, or even years, to see the good that it will bring, but over time your attitude of blessing her no

How Not to Treat Your Ex-Wife

A former neighbor of ours had an affair with a co-worker and then demanded a divorce from his faithful wife of 25 years. Like so many men in this situation, he could rationalize and justify his actions with the best of them, but he was totally in the wrong. Understandably, his wife and kids were devastated. I don't understand what the guy was thinking—he had a good family and a lovely wife, and he threw it all away for a bimbo (to be honest, that is a pretty good description of the co-worker). Anyway, his actions led directly to the destruction of his family via a devastating divorce.

You would think a guy who had brought all these disasters on himself and his family would at least be humble and somewhat gracious to his long-suffering wife and kids. But no. When he realized how much the divorce was going to cost him financially (please note: There is NO such thing as "no fault" or "low cost" divorce), he got even uglier with her. He withdrew his support for the tuition payments of their college-age kids and even had his new girlfriend break into his ex-wife's home to "liberate" some of the things he thought he deserved. (I am telling the truth here—I could not make this stuff up.) Anyway, you get the picture. The guy brought disaster upon himself and his family, and then was a complete jerk about it.

No wonder his ex-wife hates him, his kids despise him and his former friends and neighbors will have nothing to do with him. I predict that he and his co-worker lover will be history in a few short years, and he will be totally and completely alone. As the old saying goes, "What goes around comes around." In fact, the Bible itself could not be clearer on this point: "Do not be deceived: God cannot be mocked. A man reaps what he sows" (Galatians 6:7).

matter what will have positive and long-lasting consequences—not just in her life and your children's lives, but in your own life as well.

Just ask former Indiana Governor Mitch Daniels. I do not know Governor Daniels personally, but from what I've read, he never stopped loving and caring for his wife even in the midst of their very difficult divorce. Four years later, they remarried, and now they have what is said to be a wonderful marriage. I'm not saying that is going to happen in every case, but it's a nice thing to shoot for. Even if you don't remarry your ex and live happily ever after, at least she will respect and appreciate your kindness and generosity—and so will your kids.

Thank you again for wanting to be the very best single dad you can be. That is a good thing you are doing, not only for your kids and for your ex-wife, but for yourself as well. May God grant you the strength, the courage and the wisdom you need to be successful in this important quest.

For Further Reflection

1. Do you know that you are, quite literally, *irreplaceable* in your children's lives? Does your life today reflect that reality? Why or why not?

2. What kind of relationship do you have with your ex-wife, the mother of your children? What can you do to improve it?

3. How important would your efforts be to your children?

Today's Quick Wins

1. Take 60 seconds to think about the last time you had a really wonderful time with your kids. Meditate on how good that felt for you and for them.

2. Take as long as you'd like to reflect on how much your kids still need you in their lives and how deeply they long for you and their mom to get along.

3. Take 60 seconds to decide what fun thing you are going to do with your kids when you next see them—and what one thing you can do to most bless your ex-wife. Then do them both.

Note

1. Margaret Guminski Cleek and T. Allan Pearson, "Perceived Causes of Divorce: An Analysis of Interrelationships," *Journal of Marriage and the Family,* February 1985.

2

How to Handle Life's Beanballs

*Life is not easy or predictable for anyone, ever.
What you decide to do when life throws you these
beanballs will determine your success as a father.*

---

*I have learned the secret of being content in any and every situation,
whether well fed or hungry, whether living in plenty or in want. I can do
everything though him who gives me strength.*
PHILIPPIANS 4:12-13, *NIV*

*While it's true that I would never have chosen the difficult things
I have faced in my life, I must admit that they have made me a stronger
and better man than I was before.*
KEN Y., TOKYO, JAPAN

If you would like to discuss any of this material via email,
feel free to contact me at **gws@beabetterdadtoday.com**

D on't be fooled by the stuff you see on TV or the enviable image of the neighbors you really don't know down the street . . . life is not always easy for anyone. Life can and should be fun and exhilarating, and with a family it certainly is challenging. But it is never easy. Even for a kid who had it all growing up—and I know a fair share of them—life is at times bitter, sad and difficult. We are each going to get some serious beanballs thrown at us during our lives. That is certain for all of us. The only question for you is this: How are you going to handle them? Like a professional baseball player, the answer to that question is going to determine if you are going to be a major league dad or not

The reality of life is that there are many, many things outside of our control. If you disagree with me on that, just wait 10 years and let's talk again. Injury, illness and even death can come out of the blue. Companies blow up. Jobs disappear. Family or close friends let us down. As a direct result, we and/or those around us get hurt—sometimes very badly. Fortunately, there is something powerful and important over which we have total and direct control: how we respond to life's beanballs.

If you're not a baseball fan, a "beanball" is when the pitcher throws the ball—at almost 100 MPH—at the opposing batter's head. Sure it's illegal, but it happens. Just like a professional ballplayer, you have a number of responses you can take when life throws you such a beanball, but the most important thing to do, whenever possible, is to get out of harm's way. Any baseball player will tell you that the best way to avoid a beanball is to duck. But sometimes life's beanballs have a way of sneaking up on you and hitting you where it hurts the most. When this happens, just like any ballplayer, you have to pick yourself up, assess the damage, learn the lesson and move on. Let's expand on these themes.

When Life Throws You a Beanball

Again, rule #1 for life's beanballs is to try to avoid the danger whenever possible. This is always a good idea, because it is much better to get out of the way and avoid injury than it is to allow a hard ball going 100 MPH to hit you in the head. Likewise, when a woman starts to flirt with you, or someone you know suggests doing something you know isn't honest and ethical, or when your wife or ex-wife lashes out at you for no apparent reason, the best and smartest thing to do is to get out of the way and avoid getting hit. Let that attractive woman know that you are not interested. Tell your friend that you care for him and his future—and that what he is talking about doing is wrong (and why). Instead of responding to your family members in anger, just tell them how much you love them and walk away for a few minutes, if need be. By all means, don't get hit by these kinds of beanballs if you can possibly avoid them.

Sometimes, of course, you won't be able to avoid these 100 MPH beanballs, just like batters in the Major Leagues can't avoid them all of the time. Illness, severe injury or other unexpected trauma can sneak up and unexpectedly smack any of us. This is real life—and these things really happen. Sometimes, if you are honest, you will even bring it upon yourself. This was true with one guy I knew several years ago. He was so desperate to make a little more money that he consistently padded his expense report—

Overcoming Life's Beanballs in the National Football League

My dear friend Greg was a good NFL football player years ago—and in time he became the chaplain for a well-known NFL team. Everybody called him "Chap," and he was a tremendous asset to the team. He had a real gift of developing a deep rapport with the players and helping them in times of trouble (as you can imagine, young guys with lots of money who are playing in the NFL can get into trouble in a hurry). He had the support of the head coach, the front office and the entire staff. But after a number of successful years, the old coach retired. A new head coach came in who decided he needed to shake things up, so many of the assistant coaches were let go. My friend was also let go. He was devastated.

Greg could have become bitter and just given up, just as many guys in his situation would have done. He had put his heart and soul into that team for years, and the good results of his work were clear to one and all. But he had still been fired. He had no new job lined up, and his wife and children were depending on him. What was he going to do?

Greg took stock of his situation. He knew that he had done a good job—and that others in the NFL knew this as well. There were some important lessons to learn from the dismissal, and he thought about them long and hard. He took some time to re-group, examine his life's trajectory to that point, and test his life's calling. Fortunately, he had (and has) a wonderful wife and great kids who were fully supportive of him during this process.

Finally, Greg decided that he wanted to continue to be a "chap" in spite of the many uncertainties of that position. He be-gan to network and pray about new opportunities . . . and out of nowhere a new position emerged with another NFL team. In fact, in many ways it was a better position than the one he had previ-ously held. And because he had grown in maturity and wisdom through that tough experience, now when a player gets cut from the team or injured (both of which happen all the time in the NFL) Greg can share his personal experience of being cut himself and how he overcame that setback. In doing so, he has become an even better "chap" for his team, a great role model for his children and friends, and an even stronger and better man.

and eventually got fired for doing it. Despite the fact that he was a reasonably smart guy, he never had a real job again.

When we get hit by one of life's beanballs, we have two funda-mental choices: (1) We can learn from the experience, dust our-selves off and carry on with the game of life; or (2) we can pick up our marbles and go home, pouting. You know what I mean by this. Do we allow whatever happened to so dominate us that we cease to function effectively, or do we rub the hurt, acknowledge the pain, learn the lessons and get on with life? I'm not suggesting this is quick or painless; it is not. But it is a choice we must make if we are to remain in the game for our wives, our children and ourselves. In fact, a good family can help us take the latter path—the better path—but in the end, the decision is up to us. You've heard it before, because it's true: Get bitter or get better. That is one of the most important choices we all have in life.

A Personal Beanball Story

While I've been on the cover of *TIME* magazine, had my share of professional successes and even been awarded distinguished honors by members of the United States Congress, I've also been let go. And for me (as an insecure overachiever type), that was potentially devastating. But in that time of crisis, I found the support and emotional strength I needed from four related sources: my family, my closest friends, prayer and God's Word. And so can you.

Family and Friends

When I came home that evening after being let go from my job, my kids still loved me and my wife still respected me. I hadn't changed one bit—and they knew it (and reminded me of it). I needed that, not just that evening but also every day for months as I thought about what happened and what I should have done differently (short answer: lots—but that's for another book). But my wife and kids never lost their trust and confidence in me, and that helped me to look reality square in the face.

Likewise, my closest friends rallied around me to remind me that I was not a has-been or a lifelong failure. Sure, it was a real setback, but they helped me put it into the context of modern life where these things happen a lot, especially in the technology industry. They, like my family, helped me remember that my value was not in my bank account or my job title or anything material, but in my character and in those whom I loved (and who loved me). They helped me learn from my mistakes.

Life's lessons only get more expensive as you get older, so it is a good idea to learn as many of them as you can as early as possible.

As it turns out, I learned a lot from that experience that has helped me immeasurably in my life. And I have my family and friends to thank for that.

Prayer

Prayer also proved to be a great source of strength and comfort in that tough time. I learned firsthand the power of the apostle Paul's encouragement: "Do not be anxious about anything, but in everything, by prayer and petition, with thanksgiving, present your requests to God. And the peace of God, which transcends all understanding, will guard your hearts and your minds in Christ Jesus" (Philippians 4:6-7, *NIV*). Yes, I certainly needed that peace. And in times of deep and honest prayer, I found it.

Prayer works in mysterious ways. I do not claim to understand even 1 percent of its power or its method, but I do know that God, through prayer, changes hearts and (sometimes) circumstances. I know He has changed my heart through prayer, and sometimes He has changed the hearts (and circumstances) of those for whom I have been praying. One thing I know for sure: When I pray with strength and sincerity about something that is troubling me and then leave the issue with the Lord, the peace that Paul promises is there. Check it out for yourself, my friend. It works. You will see.

That is true because God's Word has not changed in more than 3,000 years. Contrary to some of today's "name it and claim it" nonsense, the Bible never promises anyone an easy life. It does not promise health or riches or material comfort to anyone, ever. But it does promise that if we stay close to God by His Holy Spirit, over time and through the trials and difficulties of life, we will become strong, mature men (and women). God does not want us, His children, to be spiritual and emotional infants. He wants us to be mature men and women who are able and willing to help others. The only way we can become a strong, mature and giving people is to go through the trials and tribulations of life and overcome them. Some trials are so difficult that they require almost superhuman strength to overcome. But, as the old saying goes, "The hotter the fire, the stronger the steel."

The Hotter the Fire, the Stronger the Steel

My dear friend Joe is a devoted husband, a great dad and has been a faithful friend for many, many years. He has a son who is autistic, as well as other children who need his love. Caring for his son has been a burden that few people could bear, but Joe and his good wife, Laura, have borne it. When I consider my burdens, trials and struggles, they pale in comparison to the lifetime challenges faced by my dear friend and his wife. Theirs is a burden I cannot understand; in fact, I can barely comprehend it. But through it all, God has helped them and they have borne it—and it has made them stronger people, better parents and wonderful friends. Just as important, they have encouraged hundreds of other parents in the process

So, whenever life throws you a beanball, do your best to get out of the way. Avoid temptation, speak the truth always, do the right thing. But when you get hit by that beanball—and we all will at times—know that God wants to use even that pain and suffering and grief to make you a stronger, better and more giving person. Again, that is not an easy process, and yes, many people choose to go down the bitterness path instead of the betterness path. But that is the wrong path, for it leads only to isolation and, eventually, death.

Let us resolve, together, that when life throws us a beanball, we are going to put it into context, learn from it, and move on with our lives as better and stronger men than we were before. It is a choice that each of us has to make because all of us will be hit by more than one of life's beanballs. That is just reality. But there is an even deeper and more powerful reality found in this promise: "In all things [even the toughest events and circumstances] God works for the good of those who love him, who have been called according to his purpose" (Romans 8:28, NIV).

That is a tremendous promise, brother—and that is not me talking; it is God's Word talking. It doesn't say that life is going to be easy. In fact, by implication it tells us that the opposite is some-times going to be true. But it does promise that God will be at work in us for "good"—and that makes all the difference when we get hit by one of life's all-too-frequent beanballs.

For Further Reflection

1. What was the latest "beanball" that life hit you with? What did you learn from it?

2. Did you decide to get better, or bitter? If you allowed yourself to get bitter, was that the right decision? Why?

3. Is today the day for you to turn from your bitterness, learn the lessons of that difficult experience, and ask God to help you get better instead of bitter? And if not today, then when?

Today's Quick Wins

1. Take 60 seconds to reflect on the last major beanball life threw your way. Take another 60 seconds to honestly reflect on how you dealt with it. Have you taken the betterness path or the bit-terness path—or some of both?

2. Take 60 seconds to think about taking a new path (if you need to do so). How would it feel to get better in place of growing more and more bitter?

3. Take 60 seconds to think of someone you know who has recently been hit with a major league beanball and figure out something nice you can do for him and his family today. Then do it.

3

Thirty Ideas for Long-Distance Dads

Being a good long-distance dad is just as important as being a good "regular" dad. In fact, in some ways it is even more important. Your kids still need your love, your support and your encouragement—probably more than ever. And here's the good news: You can give it to them, even though you aren't physically there with them.

It's hard to be away from my family for long stretches of time. It's really hard. But we make it work—and that is what really matters.

DAVE L., U.S. ARMY

If you would like to discuss any of this material via email, feel free to contact me at **gws@beabetterdadtoday.com**

Perhaps you are serving our nation in the U.S. Armed Forces and are far from home. Or perhaps you are in prison or in some another situation that takes you far away from your family for long periods of time. Perhaps you are required to be away from your family for many months or even years at a stretch, or maybe soon you will be able to get back home. Perhaps your children are going off to college or into the military hundreds, or even thousands, of miles away. Regardless of your particular situation, know that you're a member of a growing club. Long-distance fatherhood is a rising trend—and one that is going to continue to increase in the future. So no matter why you find yourself serving in the role of long-distance dad, thank you for still wanting to be the best dad you can be.

I say "thank you" because your role as a long-distance dad is just as vital and important for your children as an "at home" dad. You have the same challenges as any other dad, but with the added difficulties of multiple time zones, large distances and complicated restraints thrown in. But don't let the fact that you aren't with your kids every day fool you: Your kids still need your love, long for your approval, and look for your counsel (even though it may not seem like it at times). Your kids still need you, no matter where you (or they) are based in the world—and they always will (and, by the way, that is also absolutely true for your wife as well).

Being a good dad is never easy, but it is 10 times more difficult when you are far from your family. I know this from personal experience. One time, I was working in South America while my family was living in New York. We did that for more than a year. I got to fly home from time to time, and we were mostly in the same time zone, so in many ways my long-distance dad experience was easier than most. But it was still plenty stressful for our family, and out of it we learned some important lessons. I've also spoken with many long-distance dads who have dealt with much tougher assignments—and I've learned a lot from each of them. (I have no doubt that if you're a long-distance dad yourself, you have some nuggets of wisdom for us as well. I hope you will share them with us—and benefit from the fellowship and support of other long-distance dads—at www.facebook.com/BeaBetterDadToday.)

My experience taught me that it is even more important for long-distance dads to develop the Ten Tools of Fatherhood that we talked about in earlier chapters. Each one of these tools will be critical to your success as a long-distance dad and husband. You're also going to need extra helpings of commitment, courage and communication and special help and understanding from your family, friends and co-workers. These elements will be critical to making your long-distance relationships work.

Being a successful long-distance dad will require two additional special toolsets that we're going to look at below: one set for strengthening your relationship with your kids, no matter how many miles you are apart; and one set for strengthening your relationship with your wife. Regardless of how difficult your experience as a long-distance dad has been so far, I promise that if you use the various ideas in these toolsets, your role as a long-distance dad will become both more fun and more rewarding.

Strengthening the Relationship with Your Kids

We will first look at 30 different time-tested ideas you can use to strengthen your relationships with your kids. Pick and choose the ones that seem most appealing to you and your family—and test them for yourselves. See what works best, and experiment to find other ideas that work even better. Please be sure to share your experiences and ideas with us at www.facebook.com/BeaBetterDad Today. And remember, long-distance dads come in all situations. Whether you've been transferred to another state, your daughter has gone off to college or your son has been deployed to Iraq, your kids still need you. You can still be a great dad—even over the miles.

Ten Ideas for Long-Distance Dads with Kids of all Ages

1. At least once a week, write each of your children a warm, age-appropriate letter or email and, if possible, include pictures of

you, your workplace and your living quarters. Be sure to let your kids know how much you miss them and care about them. You can keep the letters short, but be sure to mention things that are happening in their lives (for example, "I'm so proud of you for getting an A on that test" or "I watched the DVD of your school play, and you were great!"). Even in these days of Internet communications, the written word—especially in your own handwriting—is powerful in the lives of your children.

2. From time to time, include a fun item with the letters. This could be an article from the local newspaper, your own artwork, a note from a fellow soldier or friend telling your kids how much their dad misses them, or anything else that will spice up the letter and make it more personal and real.

3. Join your family at a regular time via Skype. This is easy and free, as long as both you and your family have access to a PC (it's even better if both PCs have a camera—then you can also see each other). You can "join" your family for dinner or read a book to your kids. Just make a regular time and stick to it as much as you can. Your kids will love it!

4. Have your wife or a friend film your children's games, plays or other activities and send them to you via email or DVD. This is a great way to stay in touch with what your kids are doing, and it will enable you to compliment them honestly and truthfully when they do well.

5. If possible, do a photo or video documentary of your typical day. Be sure to give plenty of details such as where you usually eat, with whom you work, what you do at work, and how you get around. You might think these things are boring because you live them every day, but trust me, your kids will be very interested in seeing your average day. It will help them understand where you are and what you are doing.

6. After you have sent your kids a video of your own, ask them to do a photo or video documentary of their typical day to send to you. This could be a fun project for the whole family, or your older kids could do their own videos just for you.

7. Did you know that you can have a star officially named after your child? It costs a little bit, but I always thought it was really cool, and your kids will love it. Call 1-800-282-3333 for more information on how to do it.

8. If you have access to postcards, send the most interesting ones you can find—and send a lot of them. If you aren't able to buy postcards, make your own by drawing pictures on an index

I Knew My Daddy

When Todd was four years old, his dad went off to fly airplanes in the Middle East. He was away from the family for a long time, and they missed him very much. But even though he was so far away, Todd talked on the telephone with him almost every day. Todd's dad would tell him what he had done that day, and he would ask Todd about his day. Todd always loved talking to him.

His father also sent him pictures of the places that he visited and a little card telling Todd about each place. That was fun. Best of all, his dad would sometimes call just as he was going to bed. His mom would put the phone in his room, and his dad would read one of his favorite bedtime stories while she turned the pages.

When Todd's dad finally came home, he didn't really recognize him. But as soon as he said Todd's name, he knew it was him, because he knew his Daddy's voice. So he ran up to his father and gave him a big hug. Todd was so glad to have him back home with the family, and now he could read a bedtime book right next to him.

card. I call this a "postcard barrage." Over time, your kids will start looking in the mail to find today's postcard from Dad!

9. If the Internet is available to you, find some games to play together, especially with older children. Games such as Monopoly, Jeopardy and Wheel of Fortune are all easily available on the Internet, as are all types of card games and games like chess, checkers and backgammon. There are many sites (such as Facebook and Yahoo Games) that offer lots of great multi-player games that you can play with far-away loved ones for free.

10. If your family has a phone with a speaker on it, ask a family member to put it on the kitchen table while everyone is eating. This way, your family can "have" dinner with you. Likewise, as with the Skype idea above, if your kids are about to go to bed, you can read them their favorite bedtime story and pray with them (a very important practice for all fathers). You can also call them in the morning to wish them a great day.

Ten Ideas for Long-Distance Dads with Younger Kids

1. Write a letter to your younger children made out of interesting items, especially things your child likes (like colored paper in his or her favorite color). You can use almost anything: wrappers from your favorite candy, images from local magazines, or pictures of you in your favorite spots. You can also use paper that has been cut into special shapes (Christmas trees or shamrocks, for example).

2. Before you leave home for an extended stay away from the family, create a treasure hunt for your children. Hide a bunch of "treasure" (their favorite candy, short love letters, a new toy or a new book) around the house. Send them a new clue every day when you get to your post.

3. Get a picture of yourself put on a pillowcase or a blanket and send it home.

4. Have some stickers made with your picture on it and send them to each of your younger kids for their notebooks, their locker at school or whatever. If you're serving with the U.S. military, be sure to send your kids photos of you in your full uniform. Not only will they be able to proudly display this picture or sticker, but it will also help their friends to understand why Dad is away.

5. Arrange for something special (such as balloons, flowers, pizza) to be delivered to your child after a special event (e.g., a concert, a play, or a ball game). Be sure to include a note telling them how proud you are of what they have done. Or get a friend or your wife or an older sibling to put up a special poster from you to your child at home or at school. Anything that shows that you love them—and you are there for them even across the miles—will be great.

6. If your child falls ill, send a care package with all the things he or she will need to feel better and get well. You could send a stuffed animal, his or her favorite candy, a can of chicken noodle soup, a special blanket, a video with a loving "get well soon" message, and so on.

7. Do a puzzle for your kids using clues from their life and yours (for example, "In what city is Daddy living?" "What was the name of Julia's teacher last year?"). You can easily create your own crossword puzzle and then send one, two or three clues every day for a week. When they complete the puzzle, the kids get a treat (such as a McDonald's gift certificate or late-night movie with Mom, or whatever they will consider special).

8. Go on a virtual trip together on the worldwide web. Use Skype or one of the many instant messenger programs to communicate with each other while looking at interesting websites. You can start

at www.natgeo.com, www.nasa.gov or www.pbs.org, where they have loads of fascinating articles and places to explore all the time.

9. Send your kids a care package with cookie cutters and all the (non-perishable) ingredients for their favorite snacks. Most kids like to bake—even our teenage boys do it with friends some-times—and if that is also true for your kids, this will allow you to "help" them bake while you are away.

10. If you're a musician (even if you're not a great one), write a spe-cial song for your kids. You can use a well-known song and just write your own lyrics, which is a lot easier than writing a song from scratch. Get some friends to help you perform it, and then send it to your kids on a CD with your picture on it. Have fun with it, but make it personal. They will love it.

Ten Ideas for Long-Distance Dads with Teenagers

1. If you have teenagers, be sure to text or email them whenever possible. Keep it short and keep it focused on them and their lives ("How did that test turn out?" "How's your friendship with _____ going?" "How's that new science teacher?" "Can I help you on your homework today?"). They might not be super re-sponsive at first, but just keep at it. They will appreciate it, even if they might not say so.

2. Join Facebook and "friend" your teens. Don't get upset if they don't friend you back right away—these things usually take time. Also, try not to be judgmental; Facebook can be a bit wild sometimes (most kids don't control what other "friends" post on their Face-book pages). Remember that the most important thing is building and strengthening your relationship over the miles. Criticizing some crazy post or picture by some random "friend" won't help.

3. These days, most videogames have a multi-player mode that al-lows you to connect to and play with (or against) people around

the world. If your teenager is a big *Gears of War* or *Madden Football* or *Halo* fan, you can play with him wherever you are. You could even set up a tournament with other long-distance dads and their kids.

4. Write a short book of "life lessons for my beloved son (or daughter)." Every week, jot down a few of the most important lessons you've learned in life. Don't forget to write down how you learned those lessons—which will make it more interesting for them and help them know you better. Each time you finish a chapter, send it to your child. Be sure to personalize it and make it age-appropriate. Your children need to learn from your wisdom, and this is a great way to share it with them.

5. If your teenager has some big event coming up (such as a senior prom, big game or graduation party), send him or her some extra money so he or she can celebrate in an extra-special way. Be sure to include a letter with the money explaining how proud you are of your son or daughter—and how important it is to behave properly at these types of big events.

6. Together with your kids and wife, write a newsletter for your friends and extended family. You can include columns about each child, special celebrations, family events and big family news. Again, Facebook has all kinds of ways that will allow you to do projects like this just with your family, or invite other long-distance dads and their kids to join in the fun as well.

7. Email your teenagers' teachers and ask if you can do a joint school project with your son or daughter. Maybe your kids can do a special report on the history of Iraq or why people drive on the "wrong" side of the road in England (or wherever you are). This can be a lot of fun, and a real bonding experience.

8. Plan your next family trip together. Think about what you are going to do next when you get back home or when your kids

come to visit you, and get your teenagers involved in planning the activities. It will make it all the better when you do those things together.

9. Send your kids a special "I love you" message by taking out an ad in the local or high school newspaper. If you have a minor league team close to home, you can get a special video message delivered between innings when your teenagers next go to the ballpark.

10. Be sure to make birthdays special. This is true for children of all ages (and wives as well), but sometimes teenagers act as if birthdays are no big deal, especially if Dad (or Mom) is not going to be there to help celebrate. Don't let that fool you. Everyone—even teenagers—likes to be celebrated on his or her birthday. So don't let a birthday go by without making a big deal of it. It's just once a year . . . and you will never get that day back. Make the most of it.

There you have 30 ideas to help you strengthen your relationship with each of your kids, no matter how far you are from home. Some will be easy for you to do, while others might not be possible. Try to find a few that seem best for your family and that you can do. Also, be sure to pray for your kids on a daily basis. We've talked a bit about this tool in earlier chapters, but let me just say here that prayer is one of the most powerful tools that we as dads—and especially long-distance dads—have for our children. As James 5:16 teaches, "The prayer of a righteous man is powerful and effective" (*NIV*). That is true—and it is especially true when a dad prays for his children. Your heavenly Father loves you, and He wants to help you be the best father you can be whether you are living at home or 3,000 miles away. He also loves your children very much. So ask Him to help watch over your kids when you aren't there. He will do it.

Strengthening the Relationship with Your Wife

The second set of ideas that we will examine is for helping you to stay close to your wife regardless of the distance that you are apart. In this day and age, long-distance marriages are on the rise, but they

No Do-Overs

Kevvy hadn't seen or heard from his dad (whom we'll call Chris) since he had been sent to Afghanistan. He knew his dad was serving our nation and was doing some dangerous job to combat people who wanted to kill us, but that didn't calm the ache in Kevvy's heart whenever he thought about how much he missed his dad. He knew other military families with kids his own age who talked to their dads regularly on the phone, got cards and notes from their dads, and even got to go on vacations with their dads once in a while. Kevvy's mom (whom we'll call Natasha) did the best she could to keep his spirits up, but over time the boy's grades started to drop, and his attitude grew more and more sullen and distant.

Kevvy began getting into fights with other boys at school, although he couldn't give a clear answer as to why he did so. The principal warned Natasha that her son was going in the wrong direction and that she and Chris needed to do something to change it. There were plenty of other warnings from teachers, neighbors and relatives, but there was still virtually no word from Chris. Natasha begged her husband to get more involved in his son's life—even just to speak with him on the phone once in a while or write him a short letter. But nothing.

I wish I could tell you that Chris changed his ways, but he did not. He was killed in action later that year, leaving behind a grieving wife and a bitter, confused and lonely young son. Hopefully, Kevvy will grow up to be a good man—and a better father than his dad. One thing I am pretty sure of is this: If Chris had a chance to redo his years as a dad, he would. But Chris isn't going to get that chance, and neither are you or I. So let's make the most of every opportunity we get to be the best dads we can. Today is the day—and there will never be a "do over."

are still extremely challenging. Let's face it: When you are hundreds or thousands of miles from home, your wife will face a double burden. So taking extra-special care of her is really just you doing your part to help her take extra-special care of your kids.

Many of the 30 ideas listed above can help you build a stronger relationship with your family members, even over the miles. The following are 10 additional ideas that you can use to further strengthen your long-distance marriage. Again, you don't have to use them all—just pick one or two (or maybe three) that really seem good to you. If appropriate, share your selections with your wife and see what she says. Once you both agree on a few, be sure to give them time to work. Good relationships are like oak trees: they grow slowly over time. But if you tend them well and give them time to grow, they can be the strongest and most beautiful trees in the forest.

1. Be clear up front in your communication expectations. Find out what your wife really wants and needs in terms of communication. Once you know, do the best you can to arrange your schedule to meet her needs, if at all possible. If it's not possible given your situation, let her know up front and tell her why, and then see if you can meet her communication needs in other ways. But be sure you understand her communication needs up front, and do your best to meet them.

2. Remember that all marriages—especially long-distance marriages—depend on trust. Don't do anything that might weaken or break the trust that exists between you and your wife. Of course, that means not allowing emotional or physical infidelity to develop, but it also means simple things such as really listening to her when you are talking on the phone or via Skype (instead of watching the ball game or reading the paper while you are "talking" with her). It is always important to keep your promises to your wife, but it is even more important when you are far from home.

3. If your wife likes to have long talks about the kids, her health, and/or other subjects, indulge her as much as you can. Remem-

ber, this is how you give her the hug that she needs but which is physically impossible since you're hundreds or thousands of miles away. At the same time, you and she should mutually agree that you don't have to stay on the phone just to stay on the phone. Let her know that you love her just as much whether you talk for 20 minutes or one hour.

4. Agree that both of you will keep a daily journal and share it with each other. This idea isn't for everyone, but it is a great way to share your deepest concerns, fears and feelings with your wife in a way that you might not be comfortable doing over the phone.

5. If your wife likes to play any particular board game or card game (or if she is one of those rare women who actually enjoys video games), find a good multi-player version of her favorite game online and invite her to play. It might sound silly, but this is a great, low-pressure way for you to connect with each other. From time to time, you can invite the kids to join you as well. A regular "family game night" is a great idea.

6. Be as emotionally honest and vulnerable with your wife as you can. This is especially important when physical intimacy is not possible due to long distances apart. Most wives want to be their husband's number one confidante—and they (wisely) don't want any rivals popping up. Don't let anyone be an emotional substitute for your wife. Don't let that even begin, because if it does, it is not going to end well.

7. Write to your wife on a regular basis—and write from the heart. All the writing ideas that are listed above for the kids (perfumed letters, a barrage of interesting postcards, letters written on heart-shaped paper) can work for your wife as well. You can experiment and see which ones she appreciates the most. Most wives love getting handwritten love notes from their husbands, and your wife is probably in that group.

8. Plan together what you are going to do when you get home. Maybe you can jointly plan a short romantic vacation. Getting away without the kids, even for just a few days, can be a wonderful way to get back together with your wife. But even if a little getaway isn't possible, plan some other activity you will do together when you are home. A cookout, a family football game, and at least one romantic dinner out with your wife (no kids) are all great ideas. Planning fun stuff to do in advance will reduce the stress that is natural when returning from a long absence—and it will also help your wife (and kids) look forward to your return.

9. Do whatever you can to lighten your wife's burden at home. Maybe she hates taking the garbage cans out to the street on garbage days. If you have teens, make sure they are doing it. Perhaps she is worried about an upcoming parent/teacher meeting. Handle it for her via Skype or the phone. Or maybe she hates the idea of having a flat tire. Get her a AAA membership. You get the idea. Do whatever you can to let her know that you are still taking care of her, even though you are miles away.

10. Throw a surprise birthday party for her if you can't be with her on her special day. Arrange the details with some of her friends, and be sure you are "there" via Skype or a special letter when the big moment arrives. She will appreciate your taking the time and making the effort . . . a lot.

Long-distance dads truly have some unique challenges—no doubt about that. But with a little commitment, courage and communication—and the help of some of the tools listed above—you can make your time as a long-distance dad a positive experience for your entire family.

The Ongoing Fatherhood Journey

By bearing the trials and burdens of life—
with God's help and on behalf of your family—
you will become the man you were always meant
to be. This is the journey of life.

Marriage and children, and bearing those burdens over time,
are what makes a boy into a man.
JEFF B., BOSTON, MASSACHUSETTS

If you would like to discuss any of this material via email,
feel free to contact me at **gws@beabetterdadtoday.com**

Becoming the best dad you can be is the journey of a lifetime, and it is one of the most important journeys you will ever take. On that journey you will learn to be a true and consistent blessing to the human beings who most need your help: your wife (or children's mother) and your children. But also on that journey you will find something else: If you keep on and do not break the bonds of fatherhood, family and faith, you will find within yourself—with God's help—the man you were always meant to be. I know that for a fact, because it has happened to me.

That's not because I am special in any way. I am not. When and if we meet in person—an event I look forward to—you will see for yourself that I am a pretty average guy in almost every way. But I am on the fatherhood journey to be a better dad; and by God's grace, and with my family's help, I am continuing forward. Fortunately, like God's love, the journey of fatherhood is for any dad who really wants it. That includes you.

The fatherhood journey is not easy, nor is it painless, but it beats the alternative hands down. We all know men who never married, who never bore the burden of serving a wife (and children), who never paid a personal price to put someone else's happiness above their own. Or those who married and then divorced when times got tough, and then repeated the process again and again. Or those sad souls who have multiple kids by multiple partners out of wedlock, leaving abandoned children and social devastation in their wake. Maybe you are one of these fathers. If so, there is hope for you and your children as you begin to learn how to be the best father you can be. Beginning to learn and use the Ten Tools of Fatherhood, as described in this book, is the place to start. It's not too late, and your children need you.

Undoubtedly it will be more difficult for you to build those bonds that link us both to our children and to generations to come, but it is not impossible. Nothing is impossible with God's help. In working toward successful fatherhood, we will set the table for our children and our children's children. And when they take their rightful places as fathers or mothers in their own households, they will look back and appreciate any effort made on their behalf.

Also, on a more personal level, it is just a fact of life that we men almost always need help in our old age. Who is going to help us? The wife we divorced (or never had), or the children we abandoned? Life does not work like that. As my own father's life proved, a man will reap exactly what he sows. He lived for himself, and he died by himself. He never became the man he could have been. In fact, he became the opposite.

Fortunately, each of us still has time to make this choice. Now, as we are nearing the end of this book, I sincerely hope that you're more committed than ever to the fatherhood journey, because while this journey is a life-long adventure filled with challenges, it is even more abundantly filled with times of love and fun and happiness. As we go through this journey, we help those closest to us find the love and security and wisdom they need to live productive and meaningful lives, and through it, we become the men we were always meant to be.

I pray that you have been blessed in working through this book with me. Thank you for joining me. May the tools that we have discussed prove useful to you as you master them—and as you help other dads to master them as well. I hope that this will not be the end of the line, but that we will continue this journey together at www.facebook.com/BeaBetterDadToday and www.FellowshipOf Fathers.com. Most importantly, I pray that you will never shrink from the fatherhood journey before you. In a very real way the future of your children—and of all of your descendants forever—is in your hands. And, on a broader scale, the future of our world is in their hands . . . so, in a manner of speaking, *the future of the world is in your hands as a dad.*

So let us ask God to give us the strength and wisdom, the love and courage, the joy and the hope to be better dads today . . . and every day going forward. Let us put the Ten Tools of Fatherhood into practice as best we can. And let us ask God to transform us into the men He created us to be by bearing the responsibilities and challenges of fatherhood with strong and steady hands. Trust me, brother, if He can do it in my life, He can do it in yours as well.

Be a Better Dad Today!

Leading a Successful Men's Small Group

No matter where you live in the world or in what circumstances, there are other dads who can benefit by a study of this book. Getting a group of men actively involved in discussing the issues raised in this book is highly worthwhile. The interaction will not only stimulate thinking and encourage learning but will also be vital for building quality relationships within the group. Embarking on the journey to becoming a better dad will require the bonds of friendship and support that such a small group can provide.

The following are several tips that will help your group become a healthy place where sharing thoughts and feelings can stimulate growth. Being prepared for problems that can sabotage your discussion time can help you head them off before they can create an environment that inhibits interaction. Consider the following tactics.

- *Rabbit trails*: When a question or comment is raised that is off topic, either suggest that it be dealt with at another time or ask the group if they would prefer to pursue the new issue.

- *Filibuster*: When a group member talks so much or so often that others are intimidated into non-participation, direct a few questions specifically to other people. Make sure that you don't put anyone who is uncomfortable with sharing on the spot.

- *Pooling ignorance*: Try not to express opinions or feelings without having solid knowledge of the topic. If you don't have information to share that is specific to a question or opinion, admit it and offer to check it out before your next meeting (make sure you follow through). Encourage your group members to do the same.

- *Discomfort zone*: Sometimes group members may believe they are expected to talk about matters that make them feel awkward. Help your members ease into opening up. Begin with non-threatening questions offered to the whole group. If your group is large (10 people or more), consider having the members share in trios or foursomes. Also offer opportunities for members to write their answers down, and then invite them to read what they wrote. It can be less intimidating for men to share with a small group or to think through an answer if they write it down before they share it. Most of all, provide time and opportunity—with an attitude of care and friendship—as you lead, and your quieter ones will open up.

- *Flying fur*: Opening up the floor for comments can sometimes result in disagreements being aired. Remind group members that it is possible to disagree without being disagreeable. You can create a climate of mutual acceptance by encouraging those on opposite sides to restate what they have heard the other person say. Then invite each side to evaluate how accurately they feel their position was presented. Ask group members to identify as many points as possible related to the topic on which both sides agree. Examine the Scriptures related to the topic, looking for common ground that they can all accept. If the disagreement becomes a distraction, offer to talk about it further at an agreed upon time.

- *Popularity poll:* Avoid the tendency to allow issues to be resolved by majority opinion rather than on knowledge of the subject. Encourage group members to examine the

Scriptures for insight into an issue being discussed and consider any other pertinent information. If necessary, agree as a group to do more research and share your findings at the next session before drawing conclusions on the matter.

Some members may not see the value of group participation and may just want to study the content at hand. In these cases, reinforce the idea that knowledge without love, information without relationship is sterile. Growth in learning to be a better dad will happen best in the context of group interaction where leaders and group members can work together to achieve positive results. This will take work and may at times seem difficult, but the rewards will be great. Urge your group members to take advantage of this opportunity God has given them and to keep an open heart and mind as they learn to love each other and learn to be better dads—today!

Part One: The Journey of a Lifetime

As you begin this study, invest in allowing time for your group members to get to know each other and feel comfortable talking with each other on a social level. Incorporate social time as you explore the three sections in Part One. Doing this will facilitate their ability to connect and be open to share on more personal and emotional levels. Encourage group members to read each section you will discuss before each session, or allow time to review the material before diving into discussion time so that everyone is up to speed.

1. The Importance of Fatherhood

1. Why is fatherhood the most important job any man will ever have (see pages 25-27)? Do you agree with this assesment, or do you think it overstates the issue? Explain your view.

2. In what ways does our society send out messages that deemphasize the importance of fathers and fatherhood?

3. What fallout do you see from the breakdown of fatherhood in our society?

4. What is your reaction to the assertion that "you, single-handedly, can (and will) shape the future of your children and your family . . . and the influence they will have on their society and generations to come" (page 30)?

2. The Power of a "Noble Family Vision"

1. What would you consider to be some of the most important things in your life?

2. In broad brush strokes, what do you want your family to look like in 5 years, 10 years and 20 years?

3. What are you, as the leader of your family, doing right now to advance those goals?

4. What are some practical ways that you and your family members can all buy into these goals and share your noble family vision?

3. Overview of the Ten Tools of Fatherhood

1. All 10 of the Tools of Fatherhood comprise the basic skills you will need to build on your Noble Family Vision. With which tool do you plan to start? Why did you choose that particular tool first?

2. Which tool do you believe will be the most challenging for you to use?

3. Do you think your family members all agree with this assessment? If not, how do you think they would answer this question for you?

Part Two: The Ten Tools of Fatherhood

Part Two represents the heart of *Be a Better Dad Today!* so be sure to spend enough time as a group going over the concepts and Put It to Work Guides in these chapters. Before you begin, you might want to ask group members which specific tool they feel they need the most help in using and try to focus your time on addressing those issues.

Tool #1: Family First/Family Fun

1. As a child, what did you learn about the importance of family (or its lack of importance) from your parents or other adult role models? Offer a specific example as an illustration.

2. What did you think and feel when you first learned that you were going to become a father?

3. What surprises you the most about fatherhood?

4. What do you associate with the words "family first"?

5. What does love—spelled T-I-M-E—look like in your family (see page 62)?

6. How does your family like to have fun?

7. How does having fun together affect the relationships in your family?

8. What types of things do you know in your heart that you need to do more of with your family? What types of things do you need to do less of?

9. Think about your Noble Family Vision statement. Perhaps it's not down on paper at this point, but you've been "writing" it in your thoughts. How are you doing so far with pursuing your goals? What is helping you to fulfill them? What is hindering you in fulfilling them?

10. As you begin this journey to be a better dad, what would you consider to be your biggest need?

Tool #2: All-in Marriage

1. What is the key to a happy family and one of the greatest gifts you can give your children (see page 72)?

2. What is your personal definition of an "all-in marriage"?

3. If you are married, what specific patterns of thought and action have shown you to be an all-in husband?

4. What specific patterns of thought and action reveal your need to work on becoming an all-in husband?

5. What is meant by the statement "iron sharpens iron" (see pages 73-74)? What qualities or dynamics must be present in a marriage relationship for each partner to benefit from the "sharpening" process?

6. "A good marriage serves many purposes; one of them is to hold up a mirror to each other's soul" (page 73). What have you seen in the mirror lately?

7. What does it mean to "get rid of any and all competitors to your wife" (page 75)?

8 What is the harm of even thinking about divorce as an option?

9. When was a time in your life when you proved that "the grass really is greener where you water it" (see page 76)? Share a personal example.

10. What is one way you can love your wife in a way that is meaningful for her?

11. If you are a single dad, how can you strengthen the co-parenting relationship you have with the mother of your children?

12. If you are a solo parent, what steps can you take to provide a relational environment for yourself and your children that will give your family positive and godly support?

Tool #3: True Moral Compass and True Humility

1. How does today's secular culture influence a person's lifestyle choices? What would you say our popular culture lacks?

2. What is your view of the importance of a "moral compass" (see page 88)? What purpose does it serve?

3. How does your own moral compass affect your choices? How might it impact your children's future?

4. Proverbs 22:6 states, "Train up a child in the way he should go, even when he is old he will not depart from it." If you have teenage or older children, how have you seen this principle play out in their lives? (Share both positive and negative examples.)

5. Why is it important for children to understand that all actions have consequences?

6. How do you as a father consistently set the right limits for your children and apply age-appropriate discipline in a wise and effective way (see page 92)?

7. Which of the 12 rules of discipline listed on pages 93-99 do you need to be more consistent about following?

8. As a child, what positive examples of discipline did you have in your life? What negative lessons on discipline do you need to replace with positive ones?

9. What are some of the differences between the way that you and your wife (or children's mother) discipline your children? How can you be more united in your efforts?

10. How can humility help you be a better dad?

11. Why is it important for your children to hear you admit when you are wrong?

12. Why is the "10/1 Rule" (see page 105) so often broken by dads?

Tool #4: Heartfelt Love

1. Do you agree or disagree that you can't show love toward your family without commitment (see page 108)? Explain.

2. What role do feelings play in being a committed husband and father? How do *will* and *attitude* influence commitment?

3. Marital fidelity includes more than just sexual faithfulness. If you are married, what are other ways you can set the tone of fidelity in your family? (Consider, for example, how you talk about your wife to others, how you treat her in public and at home, and how you represent your commitment to your wife in front of your children.)

4. What, if anything, do you feel convicted to change in the way you manifest fidelity toward your wife?

5. Grace—undeserved mercy or forgiveness—is love in action and is a requirement for being a successful husband and father. What has been your usual response toward family members who disappoint you?

6. The way God responds to you when you mess up is how you need to treat others. What do you need to work on the most in the "grace" department?

7. Why do most men struggle to show their nurturing, gentle, vulnerable side?

8. "[Tenderness] is one of the elements of every man's soul that helps make him fully human and fully alive" (pages 119-120). Do you agree or disagree with this statement? Explain your answer.

9. Which area—commitment, dependability, grace or tenderness— do you need to work on most? Review the suggestions in the Put It to Work Guide for this area on pages 123-129. How can you begin to incorporate one of these suggestions today?

10. Where are you growing the most in sharing heartfelt love with your family?

Tool #5: Empowering Servant Leadership

1. Do the words "servant leadership" seem contradictory to you? How do you understand this concept?

2. Why is servant leadership empowering to others? What does it empower them to do and be?

3. What makes this style of leading so difficult to do?

4. What typifies your leadership style at home?

5. Jesus is the ultimate example of a servant. How can learning more about His sacrificial giving help you to be a better servant leader?

6. What small acts of service mean the most to your wife or your children's mother? How can serving her in those ways strengthen your relationship?

7. What are some benefits of being a servant leader in your home? Share a specific example.

8. How can being a servant leader with your kids help you be successful in disciplining and praising them?

9. How would your example impact their lives?

10. How does unselfishly serving your family free you to be a better dad and husband?

Tool #6: Relationship Tools that Work

1. When you and your wife (or children's mother) are having a conversation and she suddenly says, "You're not listening," what does she mean?

2. Why do you think she gets upset when she is sharing an issue and you immediately try to "fix the problem" for her?

3. What do you think is her biggest concern today? How would listening to and understanding her as she shares her concerns affect your relationship?

4. What are the characteristics of good listening?

5. What are some behaviors that prevent a person from being a good listener?

6. What do you need to do to be able to understand the deeper message behind a person's words (see page 146)? What does it require of you?

7. What are the rewards of careful listening and active understanding?

8. "Either we are growing closer over time, generating more understanding and more empathy toward our family, or we are growing farther away from them" (page 147). How have you experienced the truth of this in your family?

9. Review the tips in the Put It to Work Guide (see pages 151-155). What is one idea that you will put into practice before you meet again? Write it down and ask a member in your group to check how you did when you meet next time.

Tool #7: Heaven's Help

1. How would you describe your experience with faith in God?

2. If you don't know God as your heavenly Father, what questions do you have about Him? What stands between you and God?

3. What comes to mind when you hear someone refer to God as your "heavenly Father"? Does this have positive or negative connotations?

4. How well do you think your concept of God as your heavenly Father lines up with what the Bible says about what God is like?

5. How can a close relationship with God help you to be a better dad?

6. How can studying the Bible help you get to know God better and learn from Jesus' example?

7. What would you like your relationship with God to be like?

8. If you do know God as your heavenly Father, where in your role as a dad do you need His help? If you aren't seeking God now, will you consider checking it out?

9. How would praying for your family affect the way you relate to them?

10. As a father protecting your family, how can you combat the evil that tries to undermine and destroy your relationships?

11. If you didn't have an earthly father who provided a healthy example for you to follow, how can knowing your heavenly Father fill that need in your life?

Tool #8: Other Good Dads

1. What is meant by the statement that "there are no great 'Lone Ranger' dads" (page 184)?

2. How would you describe a true friend?

3. It may not take a village to raise a child, but it does require the teamwork of other caring and committed dads to help you become a "Major League" dad yourself. Who are the men you spend the most time with right now? Does the influence of this group contribute to or detract from your goal of becoming a better dad?

4. How do men of strength and courage exude the qualities of *competence, character* and *commitment*?

5. In addition to the members of your group, is there at least one male friend in your life who asks you honest questions about the issues covered in this book? If not, who could you ask to be that friend? Who could you be a friend to in that regard?

6. In what areas of life do you need encouragement and accountability from a trusted male friend?

7. Why is it a good idea to seek out an older dad as well as peer-age dads to help you? (Review the tips in the Put It to Work Guide on pages 190-193 when seeking out men to support you as a father and friend.)

8. What role does God, your heavenly Father, play in your life as a husband and father?

9. How can the support of praying with other dads help you be a better dad? How can prayer help you be accountable?

Tool #9: Optimistic, Never-Surrender Attitude

1. "There will be times of fatigue, disillusionment and self-doubt in our lives. No dad, not one, escapes these challenges" (page 196). Does this statement encourage you or depress you? Why?

2. Why do you need both optimism and a never-surrender attitude to be a good husband and/or father? Why can't you have one without the other?

3. How can keeping your Noble Family Vision in mind on a day-to-day basis help you keep the right attitude?

4. "Life . . . is *all* about the proper response . . . [and] the only thing you can control is your response" (page 203). How have you found this to be true?

5. What is one challenge in your life that has helped you mature as a father and not remain an "emotional infant" (page 204)?

6. Do you believe that nothing happens to you without a reason? Explain your view and how it helps or hinders you from developing an optimistic, never-surrender attitude.

7. James 1:2 states, "Count it all joy, my brethren, when you encounter various trials" (*NASB*). If you are married, what was a time when you overcame a major challenge in your marriage? In what way did it change both of you?

8. What is meant by "burning your boats" in order to sharpen your "Optimistic, Never-Surrender Tool" (see page 201)?

9. How can doing this help you persevere for the long haul?

Tool #10: Dynamic, Whole-Person Support

1. How should a husband and father support his family?

2. What is meant by providing "whole-person" support?

3. What does it mean to emotionally support your family? How can this affect your relationship with them?

4. How can you express emotional support differently for each of your family members?

5. What are some ways you as a father can *physically* support your family? How does physical support go beyond providing for basic material needs?

6. How would you describe your *intellectual* support of your family? What are some specific ways you can encourage intellectual growth in your family?

7. What is involved in providing *spiritual* support for your family? What are the biggest challenges your family faces in this area?

8. What are the rewards of being assertive as the spiritual leader of your family?

9. What can you do to be a student of the members of your family?

10. Jesus says that the second most important commandment of all is to love others as you love yourself (see Mark 10:31). How does "whole-person support" meet the requirements of this biblical command?

11. Which of the areas of whole-person support do you need to shore up with your family? Ask for suggestions from your fellow group members on how to begin.

Part Three: Special Situations

The chapters in Part Three can be used throughout your group discussions as the situation warrants based on the composition of your particular men's group. Be sure to be familiar with the material in this section so you can be sensitive to members who may be single dads, handling difficult circumstances, or parenting long-distance. Feel free to adapt questions or add to what is provided to tailor the discussion for the specific life-situations and needs of your group members.

1. Being the Best Single Dad You Can Be

1. How would you respond to the statement, "No matter what the situation, your kids still need you—and you are still their dad" (see page 224)?

2. If you are separated from your children, what are the consequences of giving up on your relationship with them?

3. What are some healthy steps you can take to initiate a relationship with your kids if there is emotional distance between you?

4. Why is it important to take this process one step at a time?

5. If you are a widower, what changes might you need to make to invest extra time with your kids?

6. What impact does it have to know that God has special concern for those who have lost a spouse? How can God be a source of strength (see Joshua 1)?

7. If you are divorced, how can the way you treat the mother of your children impact their future? How can it impact your relationship with them?

8. Why is it important to forgive your ex-wife (see pages 229-232)?

9. What changes need to happen in the way you treat your ex-wife? What is at stake if you don't make these changes?

10. What does taking the initiative in creating a healthy co-parenting relationship say about your character? What does it communicate to your children?

2. How to Handle Life's Beanballs

1. What are some difficult situations that life has thrown at you?

2. Do you suffer from any self-inflicted wounds?

3. How do you tend to react when life gets tough to handle?

4. What situations can you avoid? Where are your weaknesses?

5. How can the support of friends help you weather a difficult situation?

6. How can prayer be a source of strength and comfort?

7. "God, through prayer, changes hearts and (sometimes) circumstances" (page 242). What does this statement mean to you personally? What do you see as the purpose of prayer?

8. How can a difficult situation be a learning opportunity? Share an example from your experience.

9. What impact can growing through adversity have on your family and your ability to handle the next tough situation?

10. What are the consequences of not learning from difficulties? How can this affect your relationships, character and attitudes?

3. Thirty Ideas for Long-Distance Dads

1. What are several reasons why a dad might have a long-distance relationship with his family?

2. Why does a long-distance dad and husband need to be intentional about pursuing a strong relationship with his family?

3. How can you incorporate a sense of fun and adventure into your time apart?

4. What expressions of love and caring does each member of your family need to receive from you?

5. What skills do you need to use and develop to share these expressions of love with your family members?

6. What technology do you have available to communicate with your children and your wife? Who can help you create special memories or experiences for them?

7. Considering the ages and interests of your children, which of the ideas shared on pages 247-254 would you like to try first?

8. What kind of support can you give to your wife (or children's mother) while you are apart? Who can help you?

9. If you are married, what stresses is your marriage facing during this time?

10. How can good communication help you build and maintain a strong, trusting and growing relationship with your wife or your children's mother?

ACKNOWLEDGMENTS

The direction of a man's life comes down to a handful of a few very important decisions. The three most important decisions that I made in my life were: (1) asking Jesus Christ to come into my heart and be my guide by the power of His Holy Spirit; (2) asking Marina to be my wife and agreeing with her to have a big family; and (3) deciding to put friendship before money. Virtually everything that I have accomplished in my life stems directly from these decisions and the completely undeserved blessings of our heavenly Father.

Although there are many, many people to thank for their wonderful help in writing *Be a Better Dad Today!* it is easy to know where to start. I do sincerely thank God for His guidance and blessing. Although it is true that sometimes the Lord works in mysterious ways, it is also true that over the scope of 30 years, I can clearly see His Spirit at work in my life. And I am deeply thankful for it.

I thank my wonderful wife, Marina, who has been the heart of our family for 20-plus years. There would be no Slayton family without her. Not only has she shown our children what true love and dedication look like, but she has also helped break the multiple generational curses that came down to our family on both sides. Through it all, Marina has stuck with me in thick and thin (and trust me, there have been some pretty thin times). In doing so, she has become my best friend in the whole world and has helped me to become a (much) better man.

I thank our four beloved children for each being strong and courageous in their own way. Sasha, Christian, Daniel and Nicholas are truly the lights of our life. I thank them for being their own selves while being the soul of our family both today and into the future. I thank them for cutting me slack when I slip up (they have to use grace a lot with their old dad). And I thank them for their love for one another . . . may that never lessen. Finally, I thank them for their commitment to truth. May they never let go.

I also want to thank my closest friends around the world who have helped me to become the man I am today (still with a long way to go—as they know full well!). Each of you had a direct hand in this book and/or has labored side by side with me in other important projects. Thank you for your heartfelt partnership. Your friendship over the years has made all the difference in good times, and especially in tough times. You have been a tremendous blessing to me—and for that I will always be deeply grateful.

Specifically, I would like to thank my friends Andy, Bill, Bob, Brian, Bruce, Chris, Craig, Dave, David, Emilio, Erick, Fred, Gary, Greg, Hans, Isaac, Jeff, Jim, Joe, John, Jon, Josh, Ken, Kenichero, Kevin, Marty, Marshall, Matt, Milo, Pat, Pete, Peter, Price, Raj, Ralph, Randy, Scott, Sanjay, Sheng-Yang, Steve, Tim, Todd, Tom, Vip, Walt, Wilfred, William and Zac. Each one of you guys has helped me write this book—even if you didn't know it. And, more importantly, each one of you has helped me in life—and that you do know. Thank you.

I would be remiss if I did not single out for special thanks my bountiful brother John Murphy, the founder and president of Active Allies. John and his team at Active Allies (www.ActiveAllies.com) have been true partners in this effort in every way. They have done virtually all the new media work for *Be a Better Dad Today!*—including all of the websites and social media efforts behind it. They have consistently gone above an beyond for this effort. Thank you all so much.

I also want to thank the team at Regal for their fabulous partnership throughout this process. From the Regal editors to its great sales and marketing people to its senior leadership, they were a joy to work with. Their ideas, encouragement and prayers have been foundational to this book. Thank you all.

I would also like to thank my agent, Bill Dallas, for believing in me and believing in this book from the very beginning. Bill you have been a partner throughout this effort. Thank you.

Last but not least, I want to thank you for your partnership in becoming a better husband, a better father and a better man. This book was written for you—and I am deeply, deeply thankful to you for investing your valuable time with me in this journey. I hope and pray that this book, and the accompanying websites and tools, will be a vital encouragement for you on your fatherhood journey.

Onward and upward!

WWW.FELLOWSHIPOFFATHERS.COM